Texas

TEXAS BY ROAD

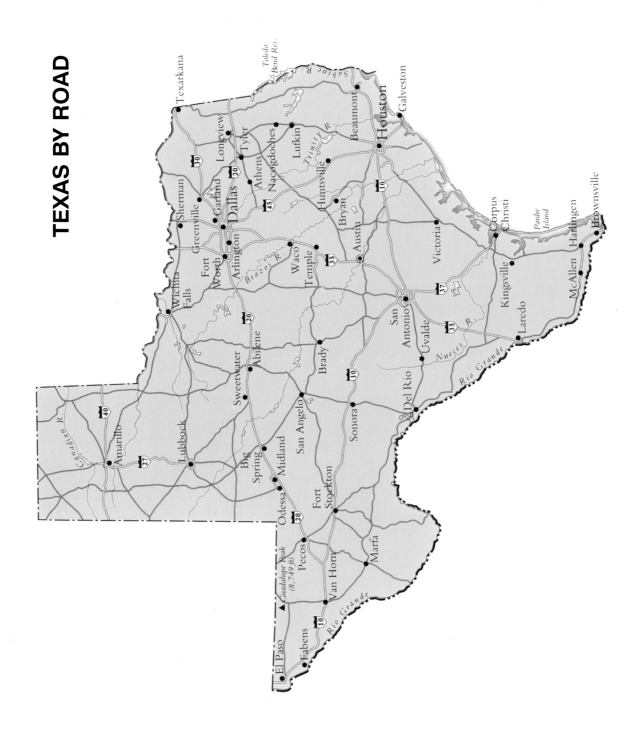

Celebrate the States

Texas

Carmen Bredeson and Mary Dodson Wade

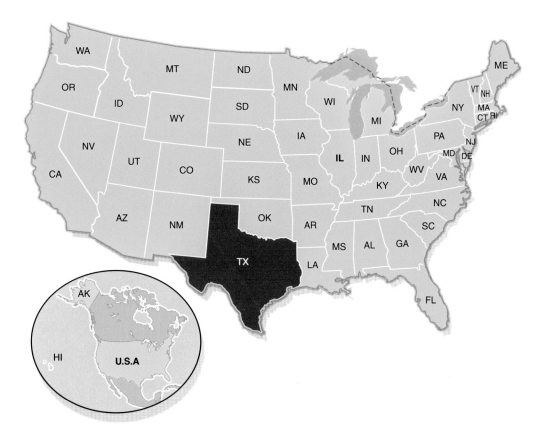

mc **Marshall Cavendish**
Benchmark
New York

Marshall Cavendish Benchmark
99 White Plains Road
Tarrytown, New York 10591-9001
www.marshallcavendish.us

All Internet sites were correct and accurate when sent to press.

Library of Congress Cataloging-in-Publication Data

Bredeson, Carmen.
Texas / by Carmen Bredeson and Mary Dodson Wade.
p. cm. — (Celebrate the states)
Summary: "An exploration of the geography, history, economy, people,
government, and landmarks of Texas"—Provided by publisher.
Includes bibliographical references and index.
ISBN 0-7614-1736-2
1. Texas—Juvenile literature. I. Wade, Mary Dodson. II. Title. III. Series.
F386.3.B74 2005   976.4—dc22   2005006457

Series redesign by Adam Mietlowski

Photo research by Candlepants Incorporated

Cover photo: David Muench/Corbis

The photographs in this book are used by permission and through the courtesy of: *Corbis:* 67; Tom Bean, 8, 92, 101; Jim Zuckerman, 19; Brooks Craft, 45; Alan Schein Photography, 64; Joe Bater, 68; Bill Varie, 80; Richard Cummins, 91, 139; Mark L. Stephenson, 96; Danny Lehman, 98; Buddy Mays, 105; David Muench, 109; Bettmann, 129, 131; Wally Mcnamee, 132; SABA/Najlah Feanny, 134; David Stoeklin, back cover. *Index Stock Imagery:* Frank Staub, 10; Jerry Koontz, 12; Ray Hendley, 14; Richard Stockton, 15; Pat Canova, 54; Stewart Cohen, 58; Kent Dufault, 83. *The Image Works:* Bob Daemmrich, 16, 48, 51, 56, 61, 63, 71, 73, 75, 77, 78, 86, 119, 121, 123; Larry Kolvoord, 24, 46, 53; Rachel Epstein, 89. *Superstock:* Tom Algire, 20; Richard Cummins, 111 (lower). *Daemmrich Photography:* Bob Daemmrich, 22, 106, 107. *Photo Researchers, Inc.:* Michael Murphy, 23; David R. Frazier, 103. *Art Resource, NY:* 32; Smithsonian American Art Museum, Washington DC, 26, 40; Snark, 42. *North Wind Picture Archive:* 29. *Bridgeman Art Library:* New York Historical Society, 35. *Getty Images Editorial:* Hulton Archive/Stringer, 36; Hulton Archive, 39, 124; Time Life Pictures, 127. *Envision:* Steven Needham, 50. *Minden Pictures:* Heidi & Hans-Juergen Koch, 111 (upper); Frans Lanting, 115.

Printed in China
3 5 6 4 2

Contents

". . . a blend of valor and swagger."

—Carl Sandburg, poet

"Texas is a state of mind. Texas is an obsession. Above all, Texas is a nation in every sense of the word."

—John Steinbeck, author

"If a man's from Texas, he'll tell you. If he's not, why embarrass him by asking."

—John Gunther, author

Texas has a colorful history.

"I am about to enter Texas—my spirits are good and my heart is straight."
—Sam Houston, 1832

"I shall never surrender or retreat."
—William Barrett Travis, the Alamo, 1836

"The most famous place is the Alamo. Everybody all over the world knows the Alamo."
—Harrison Hadland, age 10

Texas is the land . . .

"It is impossible to exaggerate the pleasant character, the beauty, and the fertility of the province of Tejas [Spanish for Texas]."
—Father Antonio Olivares, 1716

"I must say as to what I have seen of Texas, it is the garden spot of the world, the best land and the best prospects for health I ever saw."

—David Crockett

"Texas is too big a state to take in one gulp."

—*Texas Monthly Guidebook*

. . . and the people who live there.

"Good thing we've still got politics in Texas—finest form of free entertainment ever invented."

—Molly Ivins, author and newspaper columnist

"The oil and gas of the Texas future is the well-educated mind. But we are still worried about whether Midland can beat Odessa at football."

—former governor Mike White

"What Texans can dream, Texans can do."

—former governor George W. Bush

Texas is many things, but above all, it is home to the 21 million residents who live within its borders. Texans come from all corners of the globe, and each has something to contribute to the place they call home. Let's take a look at the state of Texas and at the people who make it a great place to live.

Chapter One

A Place Called Texas

Would you like to raft through sheer-walled canyons or ride horses in cattle country? How about attending the world's largest rodeo or visiting NASA's Mission Control? All of these things and more can be done in Texas.

Texas is so big that plains, mountains, forests, and deserts all come together in the state. Sharp peaks in West Texas mark the start of the massive Rocky Mountains beyond. Prairie grasses spread for miles on the plains of North Texas, while the Gulf Coast's warm weather calls vacationers to the beach. The sheer size of Texas gives it many kinds of terrain and climate.

Around 600 million years ago, landmasses called tectonic plates shifted, causing the Llano Uplift to form the Texas Hill Country in the middle of the state. Over the next 450 million years, seas covered parts of Texas at various times. Skeletal remains of plants and animals piled up on the seafloor. Silt from rivers and surrounding land washed into the waters and covered the decaying matter. Layer after layer built up, and over millions of years vast underground reservoirs of petroleum formed in the process. Oil is found in all but 21 of Texas's 254 counties.

An overlook along the south rim trail in Big Bend National Park offers a dramatic view in many directions.

Later, volcanic eruptions created mountains in West Texas. Soil carried by rivers flowing out of the Rocky Mountains spread out and formed the flat Panhandle. The edge of the sediment can be seen at the Caprock.

Dinosaurs, giant mollusks, and flying reptiles eventually appeared. The first pterosaur fossil ever found was in the Big Bend area. It had a 39-foot wingspan. Theropods (meat eaters that walked on hind legs) and sauropods (plant eaters that walked on four legs) lived in the northwestern part of the state. One hundred million years ago pleurocoelus and acrocanthosaurus footprints, some as large as 24 to 36 inches, solidified in the mud along the Paluxy River near Glen Rose. Mosasaurs (swimming lizards) made their home in the shallow pools that collected where the Dallas–Fort Worth airport is located today.

Throughout the various ice ages the continent experienced, no glaciers entered Texas. But as they retreated, warmer weather brought species of giant animals—elephants, bison, bears, and sloths.

Modern plants and animals arrived more than 11,000 years ago. Inhabitants of the rock shelters along the Rio Grande made clothes from plant fibers and

One-million-year-old dinosaur tracks, much like these, solidified in the mud of the Paluxy River near Glen Rose.

rabbit fur. At the same time, a group in the Panhandle used spears to hunt ancient bison, which were much larger than the ones we know today.

These ancient creatures may have disappeared, but other plants and animals have taken their place. They thrive in the wide variety of regions that make up the state of Texas.

COASTAL PLAINS

The coastal plains cover most of the eastern half of Texas. This includes sections of the state referred to as East Texas, blackland prairie, and South Texas. Over this large area, the climate and vegetation vary widely.

The Texas Coast

Along the 625-mile coastline, the climate is hot and humid. The upper Texas coast is the wettest part of the state. From June to November, weather forecasters keep an eye out for dangerous storms called hurricanes that roar across the Gulf of Mexico. The deadliest hurricane in history struck Galveston in 1900. Six thousand people died.

Tropical storms are not as frightening as hurricanes because they do not bring high winds with them. But hard rains can pound the same location hour after hour. In 2001 Tropical Storm Allison dropped more than 20 inches near downtown Houston in just a few hours. The costliest tropical storm in United States history, Allison caused $5 billion in damage.

Swampy coastal land is home to alligators, fish, and numerous birds. Alligators, once endangered, have become numerous. Within one week in 2003, wildlife authorities were called to four suburban neighborhoods to remove large alligators.

Eleven of the seventeen national wildlife refuges in Texas are found along the coast. A section of the tallgrass prairie west of Houston was set

Alligators are frequently found in the bayous of Texas's southeastern Gulf Coast.

aside as the Attwater Prairie Chicken National Wildlife Refuge to preserve the habitat of this endangered bird.

Coastal towns provide both commercial and pleasure fishing in the Gulf of Mexico. Commercial fishers must use devices that allow sea turtles to escape their nets. Sport fishers benefit from a program at Sea

Center Texas in Freeport that has boosted the population of redfish, a species once near extinction. The hatchery releases 20 million redfish "fingerlings" into the gulf each year.

All along the Texas coast, the Intracoastal Waterway provides a protected place for ships to sail around the gulf and eventually up the east coast. For much of Texas, the dredged channel lies behind a long stretch of barrier islands. An 80-mile stretch has been set aside as Padre Island National Seashore. It is a refuge for animals and especially birds. Much of the national seashore has no roads for tourists. But 5 miles of beaches along the northern end of Padre Island National Seashore are open for swimming and sailing.

Live oaks grow along the coastal plain. They appear not to lose their leaves each year, because some of the leaves always stay on the tree. The largest live oak tree in the state is found in the San Bernard National Wildlife Refuge. It is 67 feet tall and almost 400 inches around at its trunk.

East Texas

The deeply wooded section of eastern Texas called the Piney Woods has a milder climate. The forests in East Texas shelter deer, raccoons, and birds such as blue jays, mockingbirds, and the endangered red-cockaded woodpecker. The Big Thicket National Preserve is a unique area that includes swamp, forest, and desert. The reserve protects the unusual plants and animals of the area.

Lumber and oil are the main industries of East Texas. Originally it was the farming portion of the state. Although farming still goes on there, greenhouse and nursery plants have replaced row crops in some places. Much of the land is pasture used for grazing. Fifteen percent of all beef cattle in the country are raised in Texas.

Circular bales of hay dot the rolling prairies that make up part of eastern Texas.

South Texas

In contrast to the lush grasses of the upper coastal plains, brush dominates the southern coastal plain. Cactus, mesquite, and other thorny plants thrive with little water. The King Ranch, larger than the state of Rhode Island, occupies much of the area. It is home to 60,000 head of cattle.

Under the cactus and shrubs of South Texas, rattlesnakes slither into sandy holes. Javelina scavenge for food, while coyotes keep the rodent population in check. Fierce-looking but gentle, horned lizards—or horned toads—are found in most of the drier parts of the state. These small creatures can squirt blood from their eyes as far as 4 feet. Because their numbers are decreasing, they are now on the list of threatened Texas animals.

Deep in South Texas, irrigation allows fruit trees and vegetables to grow in the rich soil of the Rio Grande Valley. Acres of grapefruit and orange trees sway in the breeze. The Winter Garden area north of Laredo produces vegetables year round since temperatures rarely get to the freezing point.

Cities of the Coastal Plain

Nearly one-half of all Texans live and work in the large cities of the coastal plains. Among the ten largest cities in the United States today, Houston ranks number four, Dallas number eight, and San Antonio number nine. They teem with buildings, freeways, and cars. Race car driver A. J. Foyt once said, "I feel safer on a racetrack than I do on Houston's freeways."

Industrial and automobile pollution has created a smog-filled atmosphere that hangs over the cities during much of the year. Houston, along with Los Angeles, is often cited for the most polluted air in the country. Both Houston and the Dallas–Fort Worth area are under federal orders to lower ozone levels. Dallas has installed a light-rail system for commuters. Houston's High Occupancy Vehicle (HOV) lanes on major freeways cut down on cars, and the city opened the first section of a light-rail system in 2004.

A city on the move, the growing metropolis of Houston has faced its share of traffic problems in recent years.

STATE FAIR

For three weeks each October, Dallas is the site of the Texas State Fair. More than three million people visit annually. At the 277-acre Fair Park, they are greeted by a 52-foot-tall talking statue called Big Tex. Once inside, they find rides and games along the midway. Fairground buildings display handmade items, farm produce, and prize animals. During the rest of the year, the park is home to permanent exhibits, musical productions, and sporting events. The Age of Steam Railroad Museum traces the history of American railroads. The Dallas Museum of Natural History has a 75-million-year-old mosasaur skeleton, and the Science Place is a popular destination for young astronomers and those with an interest in outer space.

CENTRAL PLAINS

Huge herds of bison, commonly called buffalo, once roamed the treeless prairies and rolling hills of the central plains. In 1842 Texas rancher George Kendall said, "I have stood upon a high roll of the prairies, with neither tree nor bush to obstruct the vision in any direction, and seen these animals grazing upon the plain and darkening it at every point."

But hunters killed off most of the bison. Ranchers found the open land perfect for grazing large herds of animals. There are still nearly 100 million acres of Texas that are considered "range" land. Today, thousands of miles of barbed wire fences enclose large ranches. Winters can be cold there, but summer heat bakes the semiarid land.

GREAT PLAINS

The Panhandle sits at the very top of Texas. The flat land is an extension of the Great Plains that sweep down from Canada into Texas. The climate is dry, but perfectly round depressions called playas fill with water when it rains.

People watch the sky in the northern parts of Texas. Tornadoes often swoop down from black clouds and snake across the land. Texas has more tornadoes than any other state. Amarillo, the largest town in the Panhandle, is well known for its cold winter weather. An old saying claims, "The only thing between Amarillo and the North Pole is a barbed wire fence, and it's down." In warmer weather, the region proves to be fruitful. Wheat is a major crop around Amarillo. Soybeans grow in irrigated fields.

The area around Lubbock leads the state in the production of grain sorghums. For almost all of the last one hundred years Texas has led the nation in cotton production. Today irrigation and the use of dry farming

LAND AND WATER

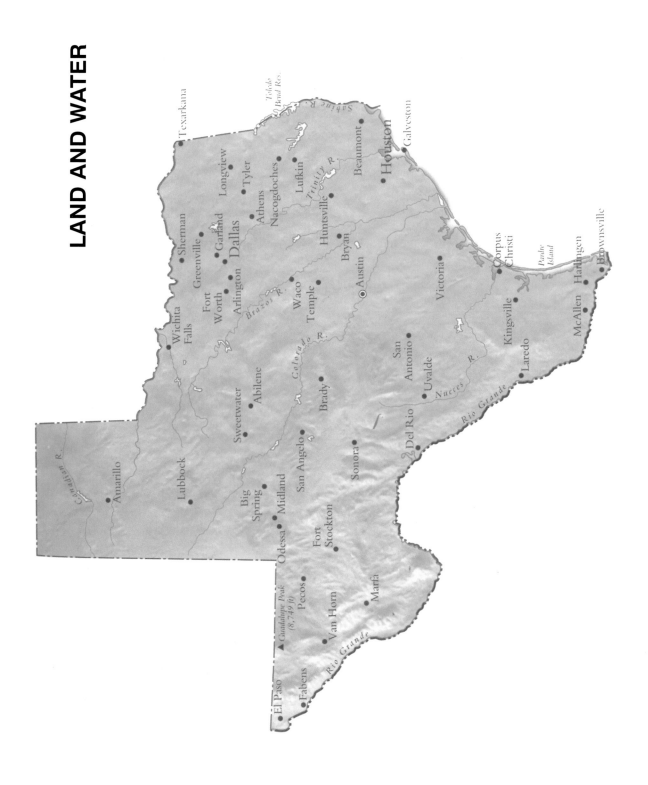

methods have moved cotton production from East Texas out to the plains. Dry farming leaves every third row vacant. Moisture that would ordinarily be used by that row is then made available to other plants, which are typically healthier as a result.

Between Amarillo and Lubbock, the Prairie Dog Town fork of the Red River cuts through the huge Palo Duro Canyon. Palo Duro means "hard wood" in Spanish. In size, the canyon is second only to Arizona's Grand Canyon. Some of the cliffs are 800 feet high. On their craggy walls, visitors can see evidence of four geologic periods covering 240 million years.

Off the Caprock, large cattle ranches and oil wells fill canyon breaks and spill onto the rolling plains. Because of the dry climate, early settlers dug wells, and windmills became the symbol of the area. Today huge three-armed giants called wind chargers line the tops of ridges, generating electricity as they turn in the ever-present wind.

The Great Plains come to an end at the Balcones Escarpment on the eastern edge of the Texas Hill Country. The Hill Country has more white-tailed deer than any other place in the United States. Goats and sheep graze on the sparse grass among cedars and

Fields of bluebonnets and Indian paintbrush delight wildflower lovers each spring.

oaks. This area is the center of the nation's wool industry. Tourists flock to the Hill Country in the spring to view a riot of colorful wildflowers, especially bluebonnets, the state flower. Farther west, oil wells dot the brown landscape of the Permian Basin.

MOUNTAINS AND BASINS

Far West Texas has more heat, less rain, and fewer people than most of the other parts of the state. Presidio, on the Rio Grande, is often the hottest place in the country during the summer. Basins, low areas between the mountains west of the Pecos River, are found in the region. Cactus, mesquite trees, and small bushes grow on the parched land known as the

Desert plants, such as these claret cup cactus, have adapted to the dry climate of West Texas.

Trans Pecos. *Paisanos*, better known as roadrunners, zoom along the dusty ground at speeds up to 20 miles per hour. Cougars, or mountain lions, and mule deer live in the mountainous areas, along with black bears, which have become so scarce they are now listed as threatened. In the high Guadalupe Mountains, elk, which became extinct in the region about a century ago, have been reintroduced, living mostly in five separate herds.

Guadalupe Peak on the New Mexico border is the highest spot in the state. It is part of the Rocky Mountain chain. Guadalupe Peak National Park is unique because it has three climate zones. Eight-thousand-foot Guadalupe Peak is an alpine forest with conifers and elk. The temperate climate of the canyons supports hardwood trees, foxes, and squirrels. The hot, dry desert floor at the bottom of the pass is empty except for scattered desert plants, snakes, and spiders.

TEXAS WATER

Texas has hundreds of lakes and reservoirs within its borders. Only one lake, Caddo, occurs naturally. The others were created when dams were built along streams and rivers. These artificial bodies of water provide recreational areas where people can enjoy fishing and boating activities. They also serve as storage basins for water that is used by cities and farms.

Caddo Lake is located on the Louisiana border. The Caddo Indians, who once lived in the region, believed that the lake was created by "powerful shaking earth spirits." In fact, it may have formed as a result of an earthquake that struck New Madrid, Missouri, in 1811. The effects of that huge quake created many new lakes in nearby regions.

In addition to its lakes, Texas has thousands of small streams and several major rivers. The most famous of them is the Rio Grande, Spanish for "great river." The Rio Grande begins in the San Juan Mountains of

Colorado, flows through New Mexico, and forms a 1,254-mile border between Texas and Mexico. Scattered small communities are found on both sides of the river. Their culture reflects a blending of Mexican and American customs.

On the northern edge of the state, the Red River forms a large part of the border between Texas and Oklahoma. Called *Rio Rojo* by the Spanish explorers, the river picks up particles of iron from the soil as it cuts through the Palo Duro Canyon. Those bits of iron give the water its reddish color.

Most of the rivers in Texas flow to the southeast and empty into the Gulf of Mexico. Along the way, the waterways pick up pollution from lawn chemicals, pesticides from farms, and toxic waste from factories and businesses. Occasionally, thousands of fish are killed in Texas rivers. Since many of the rivers flow into the Gulf of Mexico, the bays and estuaries along the shoreline can also become polluted. High levels of mercury can be harmful to people who eat the fish, shrimp, and oysters of Galveston Bay.

A rock formation known as the Lighthouse keeps silent watch over Palo Duro Canyon.

KEMP'S RIDLEY SEA TURTLES

By 1984 the most endangered of all the sea turtles was nearly extinct. During that year, only eight hundred nests were found at Rancho Nuevo, Mexico, the main nesting ground of the ridley sea turtles. In an effort to save the species, Mexico and the United States started programs to protect these turtles. In Mexico, the nesting grounds were guarded to keep animals and people away from the turtles, which can weigh up to 100 pounds, as they came ashore to lay their eggs. After the eggs were laid, they were carefully collected and taken to a fenced area of the beach, where they were put into protected nests.

When the eggs hatched, most of the little turtles were gently carried down to the beach and allowed to crawl across the sand and into the Gulf of Mexico. Scientists think that the turtles remember the beach where they enter the water and return there to lay their eggs.

Two thousand of the tiny turtles were not released, but instead were taken to Galveston. There the hatchlings were put into saltwater tanks where they were fed and cared for during the next ten to twelve months by employees of the National Marine Fisheries Service. When they had reached the size of a Frisbee, the turtles were released into the Gulf of Mexico. Experts believed that their larger size would help the ridleys survive in the wild.

So far the program is working. The number of nests increases each year. In 1999 there were 3,400 ridley nests in Mexico and 20 more along the South Texas coast. In 2002 parking was banned on a Galveston beach until the turtles hatched. The following year, the replacement of sand on eroded beaches was delayed so that turtle eggs could hatch.

Teenagers in Austin help clean up a recreational lake area.

Texas wetlands are also in danger due to pollution and too much construction. In order to educate students about the value of the wetlands, the Adopt-A-Wetland program was created by the Center for Coastal Studies. After a class selects a wetland to adopt, the students visit the site and learn about the plants and animals that live there. Other classes of older students collect more detailed information about the habitat and help conduct water quality tests. The program grew out of the simple question asked by a sixth-grade student, "How can we help save the wetlands?"

About 98 percent of Texas land is privately owned, making conservation efforts tricky. Educational programs for businesses, ranchers, and farmers teach the value of saving wetlands and bays. Some industries along the coast have joined the effort to preserve nature by setting aside tracts of land to be left in their natural state or to be managed wildlife areas. This trend started forty years ago when a colony of black skimmers chose to nest on the parking lot of one of the nation's largest chemical companies. Today two thousand skimmers come to nest each year, free of human intervention. Texans take pride in all their state has to offer, from the tallest mountains to the tiniest creatures. They all add to the rich array that makes the state so unique.

Chapter Two

A Colorful Past

When Spanish explorer Hernán Cortés conquered the mighty Aztec Empire in 1521, he established Spain's claim to lands surrounding the Gulf of Mexico. This included present-day Texas. The Spanish government sent settlers to colonize parts of the newly acquired region. Those settlers met groups of Native Americans whose ancestors had lived in the area for thousands of years before Europeans ever set foot in the so-called New World.

THE FIRST TEXANS

Eight hundred years before the Spanish arrived, the Caddo were raising beans, corn, and squash in northeastern Texas. The Caddo were related to the Mound Builders of Illinois. The remains of their ceremonial center can be seen at Caddoan Mounds State Historic Site in Cherokee County. These peaceful farmers had a complex society. They built tall beehive-shaped houses that slept thirty to forty people and had built-in overhead storage shelves.

Painter George Catlin captured this scene of an early Texas inhabitant on a bison hunt.

When men from Hernando de Soto's exploring party arrived in 1542, they met up with a Caddo band. They were welcomed with a word pronounced "TAY-has," a greeting meaning "friend." They thought it was the name of the tribe. "Tayhas," spelled Tejas in Spanish, became Texas, and the name stuck.

A much older culture had been growing crops on the Rio Grande near Presidio for thousands of years. The Jumano built pueblo-style houses. They

CADDO CREATION LEGEND

The Caddo Indians believed that a supreme being created the universe and controlled all within it. According to their legend, this god came into existence in the following way:

In the beginning there was a woman who had two daughters, and one of them was expecting a child. One day the daughters were attacked by an evil monster, and the pregnant woman was killed. The second daughter escaped and fled to tell her mother of the terrible tragedy. The mother and daughter then returned to the site of the attack and found a drop of the slain girl's blood in an acorn shell. The mother took the acorn home, put it in a safe place, and covered it. During the night, sounds were heard coming from the shell. By morning, the drop of blood had turned into a tiny boy the size of a finger. Once again, the mother covered the acorn shell when night fell. By the next morning, the tiny boy had grown to the size of a man. He armed himself and went forth to slay the monster. The man returned home victorious and rose to the sky with his grandmother and aunt. From there he ruled the world.

raised beans and squash and carried on a lively trade with other native groups. Planting crops was one of the most important skills that the Caddo and Jumano acquired. Unlike most of the other native groups, they had a dependable source of food that allowed them to stay in one place.

The Karankawa lived along the coast and were probably the first to encounter the Spaniards after the survivors of the Panfilo de Narváez expedition were shipwrecked while trying to make their way from Florida to Mexico.

Karankawa roamed the Gulf Coast between Galveston Island and Matagorda Bay. They were a tall people who wore little clothing and tattooed their bodies. They often smeared themselves with alligator grease and dirt to ward off mosquitoes.

Spaniards explored Texas—Hernándo de Soto's group from the east, Francisco Coronado's from the west. Cabeza de Vaca and his men were shipwrecked on the coast.

CABEZA DE VACA

On a cold November day in 1528, a squall capsized several small boats carrying the survivors of the Narváez expedition. The starved men were thrown onto present-day Galveston Island. Álvar Núñez Cabeza de Vaca, second in command of the expedition, later wrote, "The survivors escaped as naked as they were born, with the loss of everything." The Karankawa took the shivering men to a nearby village, but the survivors' troubles were far from over. During the following winter, all except fifteen of the Spaniards died. Cabeza de Vaca was separated from the others and spent several years as a slave of various tribes. He escaped some of the hard labor by carrying trade goods between hostile groups.

In 1535 he and three other Spaniards eluded their captors and began a journey to Mexico City. During their trek, they came to be regarded as healers and medicine men after Cabeza de Vaca used a knife to cut an arrowhead from the chest of a wounded Indian. As the Spaniards continued their journey, they were accompanied by large groups of local people who had heard of their powers.

The men made contact with a party of Spaniards in western Mexico in 1536 and finally reached Mexico City. Cabeza de Vaca returned to Spain in 1537 and wrote a book about the eight incredible years he spent living among native peoples. His journal, *The Narrative of Álvar Núñez Cabeza de Vaca*, was published in 1542.

An estimated 30,000 Native Americans lived in twelve main groups in Texas when the Spaniards arrived. Their languages were of various origins. Regardless of the Spaniards' intention to bring Christianity and European civilization to these native groups, the result was death in most cases. Spaniards brought diseases to the New World. Native groups had never been exposed to measles and smallpox. Entire villages were wiped out by devastating epidemics.

Rumors of the Seven Cities of Gold sent Coronado on a search to the interior of the continent. In 1541 he encountered the nomadic Apache on the high plains of Texas and New Mexico. The Apache followed bison herds that supplied them with food, shelter, and clothing. With the introduction of horses, they were able to dominate the plains. But once the Comanche obtained horses in the early 1600s, they swept down into Texas and pushed most of the Apache southward and into New Mexico.

SPANISH MISSIONS

In an effort to settle the territory of Texas, the Spanish government and the Catholic Church began building missions. The friars who ran them tried to convert the Indians to the Catholic religion. But ultimately the mission system failed because the Indians did not wish to live in a confined place.

Mission San Antonio de Valero, later known as the Alamo, was established in 1718 across a small stream from the town of San Antonio de Béxar. It was called Béxar in early days and later simply San Antonio. Four remote East Texas missions were closed and also moved to San Antonio. Each mission had a plaza in the center, surrounded by homes for the Indians and missionaries. Within the compound, there were workshops for weaving, tanning hides, and blacksmithing. Water drawn from the San Antonio River by

Mission Concepcion, built in 1731, was one of five missions established in San Antonio. Still an active church, it looks very much as it did 250 years ago.

means of an acequia irrigated fields where crops grew. By the 1750s more than two hundred Indians lived in each of the five San Antonio missions. That number steadily declined during the next several decades, due mainly to disease and disinterest. Spain abandoned the attempt to maintain missions in the 1790s. The San Antonio missions are now part of the national park service. All except the Alamo are still active churches.

UNDER MEXICAN RULE

For three hundred years, Spain governed the people of Mexico. By the 1800s many Mexicans wanted to throw off Spanish rule. A priest named Miguel Hidalgo led an uprising of poor Mexicans in 1810. After a decade of struggle the Republic of Mexico was formed in 1821. Texas then became part of a Mexican state and was bound by the laws of its government.

With a land grant from the Mexican government, Stephen F. Austin established the first permanent Anglo settlement in Texas in 1821. He brought three hundred families to a site located between the Brazos and Colorado rivers. The capital of his colony was called San Felipe de Austin.

In 1824 Mexico expanded its colonization laws to allow other settlers to enter Texas. Immigrants flooded into the territory to claim free land. Families in many southern states loaded wagons with all their belongings, leaving behind signs that read: GTT (Gone to Texas). Travel was difficult because of the lack of settlements. Spring rains often turned the desolate trails into rivers of mud.

TO ARMS!

Colonists poured into the state. Small towns sprang up, and cotton plantations developed. By 1830 the 20,000 immigrants in Texas greatly outnumbered the Spanish-speaking residents. This alarmed Mexican officials, who decided to let no more American immigrants into Texas. Tension between the settlers and the Mexicans grew steadily worse. Many Texans wanted to be free from Mexican rule so they could establish their own government. With each passing year, more and more Texans spoke out for freedom from Mexico.

The first shots in the Texas war for independence were fired at Gonzales on October 2, 1835, when Mexican troops tried to retrieve a cannon that had been given to the Texans for protection from the Indians. The Texans, defying the soldiers to "Come and take it," fired on the Mexicans, and the soldiers returned to San Antonio without the cannon. The Texans sent riders on horseback to deliver signs that read:

Freemen of Texas
TO ARMS!!! TO ARMS!!!!
"Now's the day, & now's the hour."

Soon, Texans were joined by Americans who responded to the call. They surrounded San Antonio and captured it from the brother-in-law of Mexican president Antonio López de Santa Anna. The infuriated Mexican leader, determined to halt the Texan rebellion, amassed an army of four thousand soldiers. In a daring move early in 1836, he forced them to march north across the Rio Grande. A rare blizzard added to the misery of the soldiers.

After Antonio López de Santa Anna was defeated at the Battle of San Jacinto, he returned to Mexico where he served as the head of the government several times.

Mexican troops arrived in San Antonio de Béxar on February 23, 1836. The surprised Texans holed up in the Alamo when the Mexicans approached. Leaders William Travis, Jim Bowie, and David Crockett were among those inside.

For twelve days and nights the defenders, and the women and children who had taken refuge with them, were bombarded with cannon and rifle fire. Then, before dawn on March 6, 1836, the thirteenth day of the siege, the Mexican army launched a full-scale attack from four directions. Hundreds of Mexican soldiers were killed trying to scale the walls. Climbing over their own dead, they finally swarmed over the old stone walls and poured into the courtyard.

Fierce hand-to-hand combat took place there and in the dark, smoke-filled rooms of the long barracks. In less than thirty minutes, all 189 Texas defenders lay dead, along with six hundred Mexicans. Among those hiding in the chapel were about twenty women and children. These included the families of nine Tejanos (Mexican Texans) who died along with the

Sam Houston had an enormous influence on Texas. He was commander in chief of the army during the Texas Revolution, president of the Republic of Texas twice, a senator from Texas after the state joined the Union, and later governor of the state.

Anglo defenders. The women and children and two slaves were set free by General Santa Anna. Susanna Dickinson, her little girl Angelina, and the family's slave Joe carried the news of the fate of the Alamo defenders to Sam Houston, who had just arrived at Gonzales.

Two weeks after the bloody Battle of the Alamo, Santa Anna's troops captured Texan colonel James Fannin and nearly four hundred of his men near Goliad. They were imprisoned for a week before they were marched out of town and executed by Mexican soldiers. News of the massacres at the Alamo and Goliad quickly spread, and many angry men left their farms and families to avenge the deaths of their fellow Texans.

REPUBLIC OF TEXAS

Just four days before the Alamo fell, fifty-nine delegates met at Washington-on-the-Brazos to draft a constitution and declare Texas independence. General Sam Houston was named commander in chief of the Texan forces. The six-foot-two-inch former governor of Tennessee was a colorful character who had lived with the Cherokee Indians.

General Houston gathered a group of armed volunteers who were ready to fight for Texas independence. After receiving news of the Alamo's fall, though, Houston ordered a retreat. With Santa Anna hot on its trail, the small army kept moving closer to the U.S. border. Citizens traveled with the army as well, leaving doors ajar and meals uneaten. Their pell-mell journey came to be known as the Runaway Scrape.

BATTLE OF SAN JACINTO

In a stroke of luck, Sam Houston was able to surprise Santa Anna and some of his troops at a spot on the San Jacinto River. The Mexicans erected a hasty barricade and prepared for an attack. When the next afternoon came without a battle, the Mexican force of 1,200 soldiers went about performing routine camp duties while their general napped under a tree. At four-thirty, the quiet afternoon air was split by the sound of rifle and cannon fire. Mexican soldiers groped for their weapons as Texans streamed into their camp screaming, "Remember the Alamo! Remember Goliad!"

The actual Battle of San Jacinto lasted less than twenty minutes, but the killing went on for hours as the Texans sought revenge for their slain comrades. Many Mexicans threw down their weapons and jumped into a nearby marsh yelling "Me no Alamo! Me no Goliad." On the banks, frenzied Texans fired aggressively on Santa Anna's men. Sam Houston rode among his troops and tried in vain to stop the killing. He shouted, "Gentlemen, I applaud your bravery, but damn your manners."

When the slaughter finally stopped, half of Santa Anna's men were dead, while only nine Texans had fallen. Nearly all of the escaped Mexicans were captured, including General Santa Anna, who was found hiding in the marsh wearing a private's uniform. With the victory at San Jacinto on April 21, 1836, Texas won its freedom from Mexican rule.

TEXAS BECOMES A STATE

Following the Battle of San Jacinto, Sam Houston was elected the first president of the Republic of Texas. Texas remained an independent nation for nearly ten years before being admitted to the United States in 1845, as the twenty-eighth state in the Union. Mexico refused to accept the Rio Grande as the border with Texas. Angered by the annexation, the Mexican government sent troops to attack U.S. soldiers along the Texas–Mexico border.

The United States declared war on Mexico. Several battles were fought before American troops captured Mexico City in 1847. The Treaty of Guadalupe Hidalgo was signed by the two warring nations in 1848.

The Battle of Palo Alto, fought near Brownsville, was the first major battle in the Mexican War.

According to its terms, the boundary was set at the Rio Grande. The United States gained the American Southwest, nearly one million square miles of land that contained California and Utah, most of New Mexico and Arizona, along with parts of Wyoming and Colorado. Mexico received $15 million.

During these turbulent times, large groups of Germans and other Europeans moved to Texas. Settlements pushed westward, and conflicts arose with the Comanche and Apache. The U.S. Army built a line of forts to protect settlers. Some of those forts are little more than rubble today. Others such as Fort Concho in San Angelo and Fort Davis are restored, and they present programs to visitors that re-create a soldier's life.

In February 1861, Texas voted to secede from the Union to become a Confederate state. Many of the prosperous citizens in Texas were slaveholders who did not want to see their workers set free. During the Civil War, Texas saw little action within its borders, but it contributed large amounts of cotton and ammunition to the Confederate army, along with 60,000 soldiers.

COWBOYS AND CATTLE

After the Civil War ended in 1865 and the slaves had been freed, many of the large cotton plantations in Texas could no longer operate. People were forced to find new ways of making a living, so a new industry took hold. Vast herds of wild longhorn cattle grazed on the state's huge expanses of rangeland in South Texas. The horns on some of them measured 8 feet from point to point.

The mural Cowboy Dance *was painted by Jenne Magafan for the Anson post office in 1941. It captures the lighter side of vaquero life. Nearly one hundred Texas post office murals were commissioned by the government to provide work for artists during the Great Depression.*

LONGHORNS

The longhorn, the state's official large mammal, is a well-known Texas symbol. The animals are descended from Spanish and English cattle left to roam freely on the open plains. After the Civil War, great cattle drives pushed them to rail lines in Kansas where they were shipped to markets in the East. Longhorns were especially suited for the trip because they had hard hooves and required less water and grass. They were on the verge of becoming extinct when a state park official rounded up a small herd and saved them. Today the official Texas longhorn herd is kept at Fort Griffin State Park near Albany. But other herds are quartered in state parks in the western part of the state. Individual ranchers also own them. Longhorn beef is marketed to people who want meat without so much fat.

Since the demand for beef was high in the rest of the country, Texans began to round up the wild cattle and move them north in huge trail drives. The cowboys, who spent weeks on the trail riding herd over thousands of animals and camping under the stars at night, became the subjects of poems, songs, and legends.

From 1867 until 1887, more than six million longhorns moved from the Texas prairies to stockyards in Kansas and Missouri. The great trail drives stopped after barbed wire fenced the rangeland, but by then the image of the Texas cowboy had been permanently fixed in the minds of the world.

The coming of the railroad in the 1850s brought more people to Texas. By 1900 there were three million residents in the state. Although there were cities, most Texans still lived on farms and ranches.

In 1901 the discovery of oil at the Spindletop field near Beaumont began large-scale oil production in the state. Over the next few years, other huge fields were discovered across Texas. Fortunes were made and just as easily lost in oil deals. Some people became very wealthy, but the majority of Texans moved into towns and cities to take jobs created by this new industry.

Then the Great Depression of the 1930s hit, and hard times settled on Texas, as it did the rest of the nation. But less than a decade later, things began to change. World War II led to full-time production at shipyards and aircraft factories. The state's economy slowly improved. More workers entered the state to find jobs.

Oil discoveries in Texas brought instant wealth to some. In the early years of the industry, there were no drilling regulations or pollution controls.

TEXAS TRIBES TODAY

Within its borders today, Texas has three official tribes. The Alabama-Coushatta live in East Texas near the Big Thicket. The two tribes, sharing a similar language, fused at the time they were living in Alabama in the 1700s. They followed game into Louisiana and eventually migrated into eastern Texas. They were not expelled with the other tribes, probably because they aided settlers during the Runaway Scrape. In the 1920s the U.S. government officially created the Alabama-Coushatta Reservation. Some tribal members live on that land today. Others have moved to surrounding communities to work but return to participate in ceremonies.

The Tigua and their Spanish priests fled down the Rio Grande from the Santa Fe area to escape the Pueblo uprising against the Spaniards in 1680. They established Ysleta, now a suburb of El Paso, the following year. In 1830 the channel of the Rio Grande shifted its course making Ysleta an island. Ysleta was originally in Mexico so the Tigua were not subject to being expelled. Their land later became part of the United States. Today at the Tigua cultural center members perform traditional dances and sell traditional crafts.

The Kickapoo in Texas are descendants of a Great Lakes tribe that was forced to resettle in Kansas. Those who drifted into Texas were expelled in 1839. Some went to Indian Territory. Others went to Mexico, where they still live. They spend part of the year as migrant workers but return to their Mexican home the rest of the year. Some camp under the international bridge between Piedras Negras and Eagle Pass. In 1983 the Kickapoo were given dual citizenship by Mexico and the United States and cross the border freely. This branch of the Kickapoo interacts very little with outsiders. As a result, they have maintained their customs and traditions more successfully than other tribes.

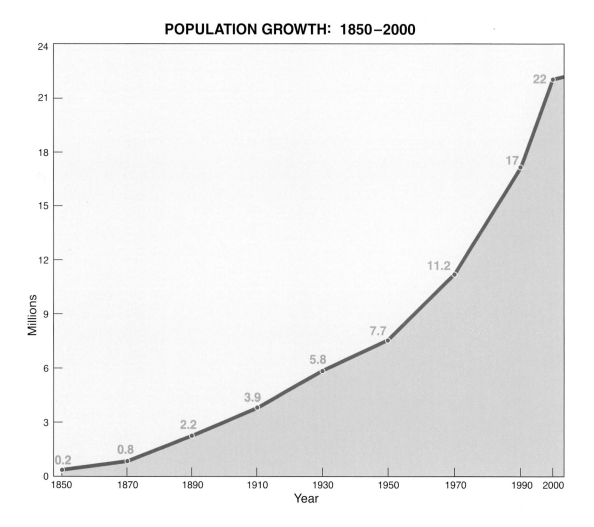

POPULATION GROWTH: 1850–2000

Millions

Year

0.2   0.8   2.2   3.9   5.8   7.7   11.2   17   22

1850 1870 1890 1910 1930 1950 1970 1990 2000

After the Russians put a person in space, the United States entered the space race. The National Aeronautics and Space Administration (NASA) build its headquarters just south of Houston. At the Lyndon B. Johnson Space Center, named for the Texan who became president in the 1960s, astronauts train for missions in space. Visitors walk around huge rockets, peek inside the small capsules that carried America's first astronauts into space during the 1960s, and watch Mission Control at work. In 1969

Americans cheered as they heard astronaut Neil Armstrong say, "Houston, Tranquility Base here. The Eagle has landed." Then in 2003, the nation grieved when the shuttle *Columbia* broke up over Texas just minutes before touchdown.

Another president from Texas, George W. Bush, was in the White House by that time. He had been elected governor of Texas in 1994 and immediately pushed for education reforms that would lift people out of poverty. His program required children to be reading at grade level by third grade and provided training for teachers in new techniques to help students learn. Because of his election to the presidency in 2000, he did not complete his second term as governor.

More than 21 million people lived in Texas at the beginning of the new millennium. The state ranked second only to California as the fastest grow-

ing in the nation. Its population swelled with births and people moving into the state. Today Texas legislators wrestle with the state's growing debt as they try to meet the needs of all its citizens. But like all the other challenges the state has faced through the years, Texans always find a way of overcoming problems.

George W. Bush and his father, George H. W. Bush, became the second father-and-son pairing in U.S. history to have both served as president. The elder Bush made a fortune in Texas oil, while his son amassed wealth through his ownership of the Texas Rangers baseball team.

Chapter Three

A Patchwork of Cultures

Texas is like a great big patchwork quilt whose scraps have been stitched together to form a vibrant and diverse whole. Large numbers of Hispanics and blacks, as well as people of other cultures, give Texas one of the most varied populations of any state. The Institute of Texan Cultures in San Antonio has permanent exhibits of twenty-six cultural and ethnic groups within the state. The Texas quilt tells a story of struggle and accomplishment, repression and disappointment, success and hope.

The image that helped define Texas in the eyes of the world is the cowboy, alone on the range with his longhorn cattle and his campfire. There are still many places in the Lone Star State where cowboys oversee herds of livestock. Modern cowboys might use a jeep or helicopter to survey the cattle or have a cellular phone to call folks back at ranch headquarters. But the first cowboys were vaqueros, *vaca* being the Spanish word for "cow."

THE SPANISH CONNECTION

Many Spaniards living in Mexico intermarried with the state's original inhabitants to form a culture we call Hispanic. The earliest settlers in

Mexican Americans celebrate Diez y Seis de Septembre, *or the Sixteenth of September, to honor Mexican independence from Spain.*

Girls from Mexico and some Central American countries celebrate their fifteenth birthdays with an elaborate party called a quinceanera.

Texas were Hispanics who moved across the Rio Grande. About one-third of the people living in Texas today are of Hispanic origin. They are the fastest-growing segment of the population. Estimates are that by 2025 they will outnumber all other ethnic groups in the state. They are already the largest ethnic group in Houston, Dallas, San Antonio, and El Paso.

Although the Rio Grande forms a barrier between Texas and Mexico, it has never been able to contain the culture of either area. In towns on both sides of the river, people speak Spanish, English, or a mixture of both. Open-air markets display colorful piñatas and pottery, along with bright red bunches of chili peppers that are guaranteed to wake up the taste buds.

The influence of Hispanic culture does not stop in South Texas but extends into all parts of the state. Tejano music fills the airwaves. Houston, San Antonio, and El Paso stage large Cinco de Mayo (May 5) celebrations as Hispanics in Texas honor the Mexican defeat of French forces in 1862.

Hungry Texans order big, steaming plates of enchiladas and fajitas at their favorite restaurants. While they eat the spicy Mexican food, a group of mariachi might wander by and serenade the diners with a lively song, such as *"Jarabe Tapatio,"* the Mexican Hat Dance.

Many Hispanics live in South Texas, especially in towns along the Rio Grande. Unemployment is high in the border towns. In 2000 Texas had an overall unemployment rate of 4 percent. In Presidio County it was 23 percent. Three years later, when hard times pushed statewide unemployment to 6.7 percent, Presidio County's rate was still three times that of the state average.

High unemployment only deepens the poverty that threatens this region of Texas. As many as half of the state's Hispanic children are

PEDERNALES RIVER CHILI

Chili is the official state dish of Texas. Many chili cooks carefully guard their recipes. Some even make the bold claim that chili with beans isn't even chili at all. Down near Big Bend, the little town of Terlingua is the scene of wild parties when they stage chili cook-offs every year. Thousands of people come to the ghost town to eat chili and have fun.

This chili was served on the Hill County ranch of former president Lyndon Johnson.

Pedernales River Chili
4 pounds of ground beef
1 large onion, chopped
2 cloves of garlic, crushed
1 teaspoon of oregano
1 teaspoon of ground cumin seeds
6 teaspoons of chili powder
2 16-ounce cans of tomatoes
2 cups of hot water
salt and pepper to taste

Ask an adult to help you brown the meat along with the onions and garlic. Drain the grease. Add the rest of the ingredients and bring to a boil. Lower the heat and simmer for an hour, covered.

born into poverty. Children often have to quit school to help support their families, so the school dropout rate among Hispanic students is extremely high.

Relations between the police and the Hispanic community are often tense. In most Texas cities, the majority of police officers is white. They may lack knowledge of the language and culture. Riots erupted in Houston in 1977 when a Hispanic prisoner was killed while in police custody. Guadalupe Quintanilla, a woman who did not learn English until she was twenty-eight years old, approached police with the idea of teaching officers about Hispanics. She developed a highly successful training program that included street Spanish and knowledge about Hispanic culture. Some officers learned for the first time that confusion with names resulted from Hispanics placing their mother's name after their surname. This training program has been used across the nation.

A fishing trip provides the perfect opportunity for this grandfather to spend time with his grandson.

Bilingual education in Texas schools is an issue that spurs debate. While some people want to see only English spoken, others feel differently. They believe that a child can learn more easily when taught in his or her native tongue, and that English can come later. Teacher Linda Velasquez says, "The idea is to get them educated, not just to learn English." Sandra, one of the top graduates of a Houston high school in 2003, was a native of Mexico who credited her English-as-a-second-language teacher as the person who helped her most.

UP FROM SLAVERY

Many of the people living in the inner cities of Texas are black. They make up almost 12 percent of Texans. The state's first black residents arrived with the initial Spanish expedition. One of Cabeza de Vaca's three surviving companions was a Moroccan slave named Estevanico. Many black Texans are descended from slaves brought to work on cotton plantations in the mid-1800s. Their songs and rhythms became the basis of gospel and blues music. Composer Scott Joplin, born in Cave Springs, gained fame for creating the syncopated rhythms of ragtime.

Although Abraham Lincoln freed the slaves on January 1, 1863, most of the 200,000 slaves in Texas did not find out about it until June 19, 1865. On that day, General Gordon Granger landed in Galveston with 1,800 Union troops and read the Emancipation Proclamation. Ever since, the day has been known as Juneteenth. It is celebrated with parades in Texas cities such as Houston, Dallas, Fort Worth, San Antonio, and Austin. During the festivities, families and friends often gather together to eat and socialize. They listen to speeches and music. At the end of the day, fireworks light up the sky.

Juneteenth, marking the day Texas slaves learned of their freedom, is celebrated in cities across the state with parades, speeches, and picnics.

A son helps his mother pick wildflowers from a field bursting with blooms.

The end of slavery, however, did not bring the end of hardship. Young men, of all races, had difficulty finding work. Some drifted west and became cowboys. Many blacks worked on ranches and made trail drives. Bose Ikard was nineteen years old when he went to work for Charles Goodnight. The two were friends until Ikard's death many years later. Goodnight said of Ikard, "I have trusted him farther than any living man. He was my detective, banker, and everything else in Colorado, New Mexico, and the other wild country I was in."

Many freed slaves stayed where they were and worked as sharecroppers. They lived in poorly constructed houses and received only a portion—or share—of the crops. This arrangement usually left them in debt. If they took other jobs, their wages were not equal to what whites earned doing the same thing. Separate schools, waiting rooms, and railroad cars kept them segregated. When an East Texas farm girl named Bessie Coleman wanted to learn to fly an airplane, she had to go to France. She become the first black person to hold an international pilot's license.

THE EUROPEAN PRESENCE

A large number of Texans trace their roots to European ancestors. Their recipes, songs, and memories have been woven together to help form the fabric of Texas.

In the mid-1840s the largest group, about 6,000 immigrants, arrived from Germany. They had come to Texas to escape the political situation in their homeland. They settled principally at New Braunfels and Fredericksburg. They built wood and stone houses that families still inhabit. They also brought the Christmas traditions of decorating fir trees and of children eagerly waiting for Saint Nikolaus. Oktoberfest is another celebration they introduced to their new homeland.

German Texans honor and celebrate their culture with festivals such as Oktoberfest where traditional music, singing, and dancing are the rule.

EASTER FIRES

Early German settlers who went to the Fredericksburg area found Comanche Indians living on land they thought they had bought. John Meusebach, a leader of the colony, made a treaty with the Comanche. A copy of it hangs in the Texas State Archives. It is unusual because it is one of the few treaties in American history that both sides kept. In 1996 Comanches came from Oklahoma to help Fredericksburg celebrate its one hundred fiftieth anniversary. More than fifty years ago, the townspeople of Fredericksburg began holding a pageant on the night before Easter that tells the story of that historic meeting.

Other western European cultures such as Swedish, Norwegian, Wend, Swiss, Danish, Dutch, French, and Belgian brought their distinctive food and customs as well. Many Swedes came to Texas to work for wealthy S. M. Swenson. The SMS Ranch in West Texas is now divided into four ranches but still owned by the family. The world's largest amateur rodeo, organized on the SMS, is held at Stamford each Fourth of July weekend. Another group, the Cajuns, descendants of the French Acadians sent to Louisiana in the 1700s, moved into southeastern Texas bringing their distinctive language, spicy food, and zydeco music with them.

Irish immigrants settled in groups near San Patricio and near Refugio, but immigrants from Scotland came as individuals or family units. Jesse Chisholm, of Scots-Cherokee heritage, is known for the cattle trail that bears his name.

Many European immigrants found work in Texas's ranching and herding industry. Colorful accounts of their lives fed the romantic image of the Texas cowboy, long in the saddle.

Eastern Europeans such as Czech, Hungarian, and Polish immigrants sought refuge from oppressive governments. The Czechs were farmers who liked the good soil of the upper coastal plain. They gave Texans *kolaches,* small pastries filled with poppy seed, fruit, or meat. The highly decorated "painted churches" in Fayette County are beautiful examples of their art. Their lively polkas influenced other groups living in the state. Hispanics adopted the polka sound into their music to create the distinctive style known as *conjunto.*

Italians and Greeks arrived from the Mediterranean area. The first Italians settled in the Brazos River valley near Bryan. Greeks congregated in cities. Houston's Annunciation Greek Orthodox Cathedral became the center of Greek Orthodoxy in Texas. Members celebrate their culture with a huge Greek festival each year.

ETHNIC TEXAS

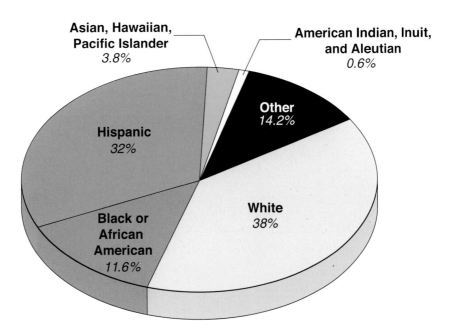

Asian, Hawaiian, Pacific Islander
3.8%

American Indian, Inuit, and Aleutian
0.6%

Other
14.2%

Hispanic
32%

White
38%

Black or African American
11.6%

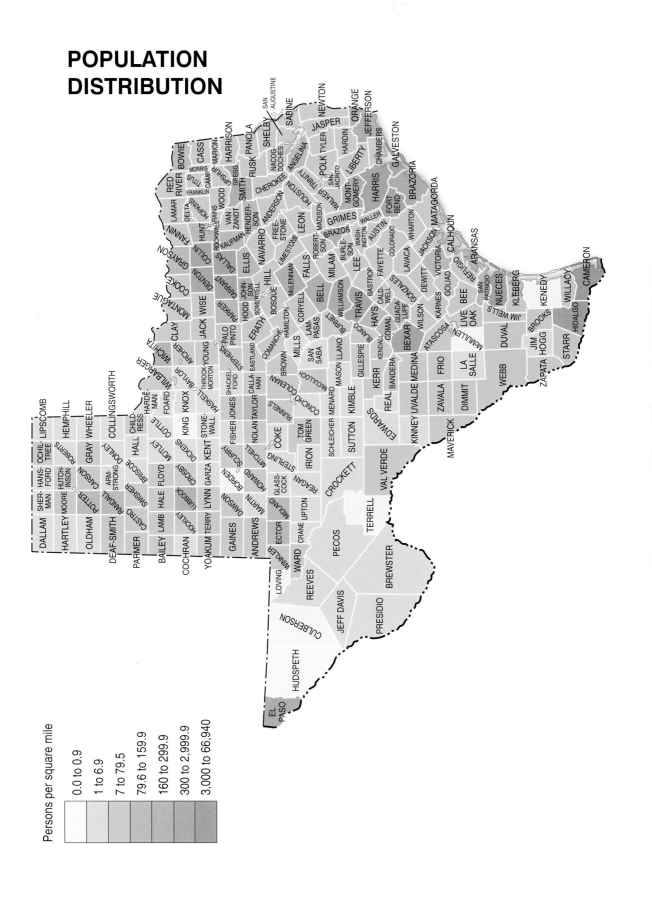

POPULATION DISTRIBUTION

Persons per square mile

| 0.0 to 0.9 | 1 to 6.9 | 7 to 79.5 | 79.6 to 159.9 | 160 to 299.9 | 300 to 2,999.9 | 3,000 to 66,940 |

Asians never matched the number of Europeans who came to Texas because immigration quotas barred their entrance for many years. The first Chinese in Texas came in the 1870s to build the railroad across the state. Today the state's Asian residents have settled mostly in cities, building temples and cultural centers to preserve their heritage.

People fleeing from communist governments in Korea, Vietnam, Laos, and Cambodia in the 1960s settled in coastal towns where the climate and fishing industry were similar to their homeland. People who came from India were usually professionals who entered universities or worked as engineers. A number of Filipino nurses have arrived over the years to work at Texas medical centers.

These Vietnamese-American fifth graders study fossils on a field trip near Austin.

A Japanese lawyer tripled the production of Texas rice in the early 1900s when he introduced rice from his homeland and brought families to cultivate the rice fields in southeastern Texas. During World War II, Texas had three camps to house Japanese Americans who were forced from their homes on the West Coast. Some chose to stay. Those who arrive today often settle in or near small, tight-knit communities in cities. The Japanese are well-known for their artistic gardens. Japanese public gardens were created in San Antonio, Austin, and Fort Worth. The country of Japan also created a peace garden in Fredericksburg at the museum honoring Fleet Admiral Chester Nimitz, commander of the Pacific fleet in World War II.

NEW FACES

The Texas quilt will never really be finished. One school principal remarked, "I have a mini-United Nations in my school." Each year brings new residents to the state. Along with them come traditions that gradually seep into the patterns of daily Texas life. As the Texas Economic Development slogan says, "Texas, it's a whole other country."

Texas is an ever-changing place. The one thing that joins all its residents is their pride in being Texans. It is the common thread that runs through the history of the state and makes the fabric of Texas strong.

Young women perform traditional Indian and South Asian dances at San Antonio's Texas Folklife Festival.

Chapter Four

A Government of the People

Whether Texans live in large urban areas or in small towns, they rely on their local governments to provide services to make their lives better. The Texas constitution sets up a way to conduct civic affairs in an organized manner. It calls for various officials, outlines their duties, and dictates how the government will operate.

LOCAL GOVERNMENT

Most Texans live in towns and cities. Many of these communities choose to elect a mayor and city council to make decisions for the community. The city council decides how to spend the local tax dollars for projects such as paving streets. Sometimes, larger Texas cities choose to have a city manager. Citizens elect the council, and the council appoints a city manager to run the community's affairs.

Lady Liberty stands atop the Texas capitol, built in 1888 of Texas pink granite. The original wooden statue was replaced during the renovation for the landmark's one hundredth birthday.

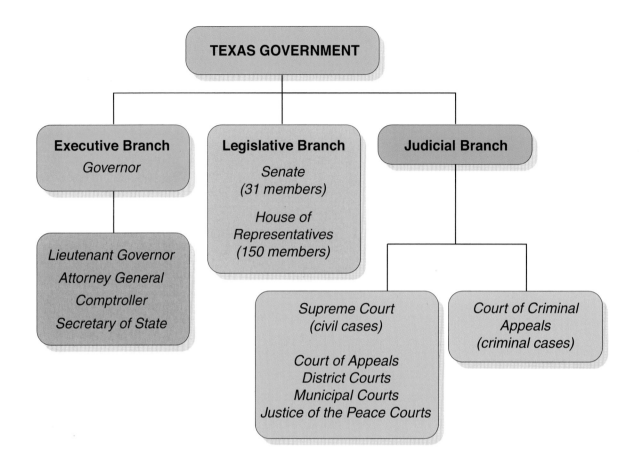

THREE BRANCHES

Under the Texas constitution, state government is divided into three branches: legislative, executive, and judicial.

Legislative Branch

The legislative body makes laws for the people of Texas. The Texas legislature has two houses—the senate and the house of representatives. There are 31 members of the senate and 150 members of the house of representatives.

LEGISLATORS, GOVERNORS, AND PRESIDENTS

In 1966 Barbara Jordan became the first black woman elected to the Texas senate. Before the legislative session started, someone asked Jordan if she was scared. She replied, "I have a tremendous amount of faith in my own capacity. I know how to read and write and think, so I have no fear." After serving in the senate, Barbara Jordan became the first Texas woman elected to the U.S. House of Representatives. In 1974 she said, "My faith in the Constitution is whole, it is complete, it is total."

Lyndon B. Johnson, pictured below, served as a U.S. representative and senator before becoming vice president. He became the thirty-sixth U.S. president in 1963 when John F. Kennedy was assassinated. Johnson was known for his hard work and long days at the office. He once said, "I seldom think of politics more than eighteen hours a day."

George H. W. Bush, originally from Massachusetts, moved to Texas after World War II. He was elected to the U.S. House of Representatives, then served eight years as vice president before being elected the forty-first president in 1988.

Kay Bailey Hutchison of Dallas became the first Texas woman elected to the Senate.

George W. Bush, son of the former president, grew up in Midland. He was governor from 1994 until he was elected the forty-third U.S. president in 2000.

Important decisions affecting all Texans are made in the chamber of the state's house of representatives.

Members of the house of representatives are elected every two years. Senators serve four-year terms, but only half of them are elected at a time. Staggered elections ensure that each session has some senators who have been there before.

On the second Tuesday of January of odd-numbered years, the Texas legislature convenes in Austin. During the next 140 days, the legislators study matters such as the budget, education, and crime. Their goal is to make Texas a better place to live. They have strong debates as they try to decide the best way to spend the money in the state treasury. Current programs are examined to see if they are effective and if any changes need to be made. Legislators also find the funding for new programs they wish to start.

If the legislators do not finish in the 140 days, the governor can call them back to finish a task. Most of the legislators have other jobs when the legislature is not in session. There is usually a big rush at the end of the session to finish their work.

Proposals about things that need to be changed in the government are called bills. When a new bill is introduced in the house of representatives, the members talk about the good and bad points of the idea. After the debate is finished, each representative votes on the bill. If more than half of the members vote yes, the bill passes. It then moves on to the senate, where it is also discussed and put up for a vote. Sometimes the two houses do not agree on what should be in the bill. They then try to work out their differences. Otherwise the bill may not pass.

When a bill passes in the senate, it is then sent to the governor. The governor decides whether or not to sign it into law. Sometimes the governor does not agree with the bill and vetoes it. If legislators still want the bill to become law, they can vote again. If two-thirds of them vote for the bill, it will become law.

The governor of Texas is elected to a four-year term. Texas governors are not nearly as powerful as governors in other states. The constitution allows the governor to appoint only one state official—the secretary of state. The citizens elect all other state officials. These other state office holders do not have to agree with the governor or even belong to the same political party.

The governor is responsible for preparing the budget for the state. Often during the election campaign, the governor promises to do specific things if elected. In order to fulfill the promises, the governor supports certain legislation. Some members of the legislature may not agree with the governor's plans and will refuse to vote for the bills the governor wants. The governor must work with these legislators and make compromises in order to accomplish goals.

The lieutenant governor is another key position in the executive branch. This officer presides over the senate. The lieutenant governor is the one who decides which bills come before the legislature for a vote.

Judicial Branch

The laws of Texas are enforced by the judicial branch of the government. Every town in Texas has at least one municipal court. The municipal court tries civil cases in which someone has broken a city ordinance.

Every county in Texas has at least one justice of the peace and one county judge. The justice of the peace can marry people, issue search warrants and arrest warrants, and can try minor criminal cases. The county judge tries more serious criminal cases. Sometimes the county judge hears cases brought by a person who feels the justice of the peace had not been fair.

Texas also has district courts. Each court covers a specific part of the state. They hear civil cases such as divorces and disputes over large

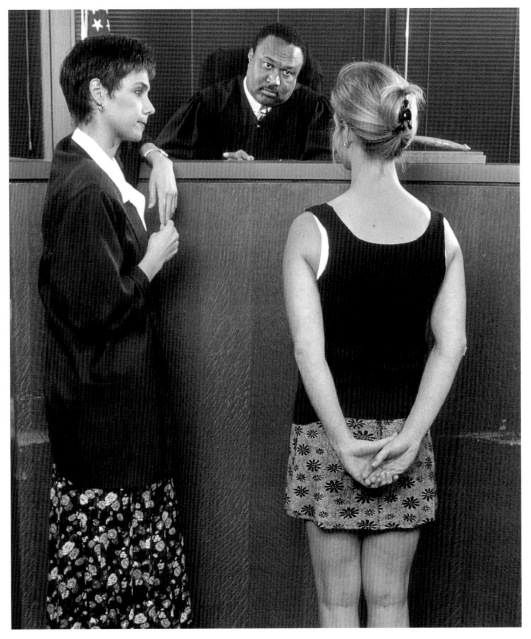

Texas's vast court system hears a variety of cases. Judges attempt to accurately interpret and apply the law.

amounts of money. They also try cases involving serious crimes. In counties that have large populations, district courts are often separated according to the type of case, such as juvenile courts or family law courts.

If some legal mistake has been made in a trial, the person convicted by a lower court can appeal to one of the courts of appeal. A presiding judge and at least two other judges review the case. No witnesses appear at these trials. The question to be decided is whether the law has been correctly applied.

Unlike the federal government, which has one Supreme Court, Texas has two high courts. Each has a chief justice and eight judges. The Texas supreme court rules only on civil cases. The top state court for criminal cases is the Texas court of criminal appeals.

TOUGH ON CRIME

Texans tend to be tough on crime. The state ranks second in population but eighth in crime overall. In 1991 Texas had to release many inmates because of overcrowded prisons. The state built more facilities and began an aggressive program to put offenders behind bars. In addition, in 1995, the Texas legislature passed a law that allows juveniles to be tried as adults at age fourteen in cases of capital murder and first-degree felony. Texas law provides for the death penalty, and this has caused protests by those opposed to this type of punishment.

The Texas Youth Commission is responsible for the fifteen institutions that house juveniles convicted of violent crimes. Of the 2,500 juvenile inmates in 2002, 90 percent were male. Nearly half were members of gangs, and more than half needed serious drug treatment. An overwhelming majority came from broken homes.

Poverty and a lack of education contribute to teen crime. The Windham School District was created so that offenders aged ten to twenty-one

Many Texans are committed to upholding the peace. A trooper with the Texas Department of Transportation hugs her daughter after receiving her commission.

could attend classes while in jail. The goal is to provide skills that will keep juveniles from repeating actions that landed them in prison in the first place. A new mentoring program helps those who have been released to stay out of trouble.

Social workers use positive programs such as the murals painted at the Gainesville State School facility to help instill pride. Poetry and creative writing are encouraged. One student wrote:

Razor wire, metal doors,
Orange vest and cement floors.
Never talking, looking down,
On every face there is a frown.

So I suggest to one and all
Stand up straight stand up tall
Open your eyes and see the light
Set your goals to higher heights
And make a difference in your ways
Or in a cell you'll spend your days.

Cities focus efforts on keeping teens out of trouble. San Antonio has participated in the Urban smARTS program since 1993 to steer youngsters away from crime. One participant wrote, "Before I started the program, I was hanging out with the wrong crowd and getting into trouble. Now I do better in school and see myself as an artist."

Many Texas cities have teen curfews. In places such as Houston, Dallas, and San Antonio, those younger than seventeen cannot be out in public between midnight and 6 a.m. Minors who are caught can be be arrested, charged with a class C misdemeanor, and fined from $50 to $500. Objections to the curfew come from those who feel it restricts young people who have a legitimate reason to be out at that time. Still Texas lawmakers want to keep the state's future, its young people, as safe as they can be.

Many police officers reach out to the community, attempting to build good relations with residents. The increased visibility helps young people realize that the police force is there to protect and assist all Texans.

TEXAS RANGERS

Early colonists in Texas faced hostile Indians, thieves, and bandits. Stephen F. Austin created "ranging companies" in 1826 to guard the settlers. As the only real lawmen in Texas for many years, the rangers earned the reputation of being tough and effective. To qualify as a Texas Ranger, it was said that a man had to "ride like a Mexican, track like a Comanche, shoot like a Kentuckian and fight like the devil." Indeed, Mexican bandits called them *Los Tejanos Diablos,* or the Texan devils.

Rangers assist local sheriffs and police in tough situations. Today, 114 Rangers, including two women, are organized into six companies. They wear no special uniforms, other than a white cowboy hat, western boots, and their badge. As part of the Texas Department of Public Safety, their jurisdiction covers the entire state. During their long history, they have helped put an end to the careers of outlaws such as Sam Bass and Bonnie (Parker) and Clyde (Barrow).

SCHOOLS

Texas spends $25 million a year to educate four million students in 1,027 public school districts. In addition, some students attend either private or charter schools, or they may be home schooled. School curriculum has been standardized since the 1980s to assure that students receive the same level of education. Students must pass a state examination in order to graduate.

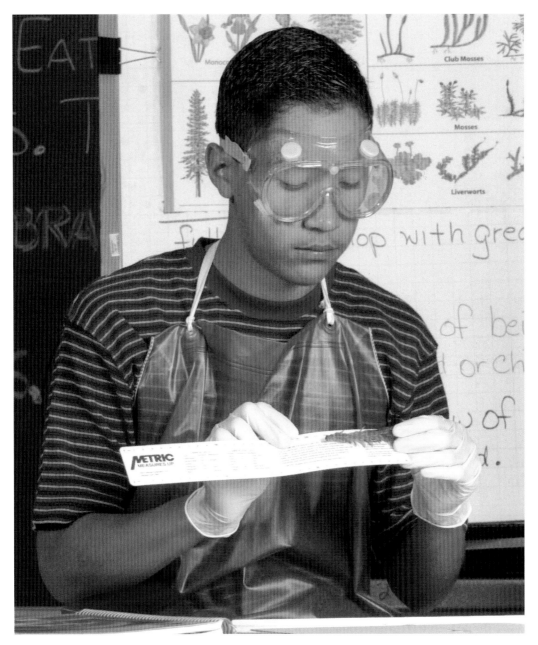

As part of a science class, this eighth grader is conducting an experiment in botany. He is measuring a piece of fern.

An after-school track meet.

Public education began when Texas was a republic. The government set aside fifty-two million acres of public land to fund schools. Money from sale of the land went into the Permanent School Fund, and oil revenues are added to that. For nearly a century the fund has provided Texas students with free textbooks.

Still, homeowners pay high taxes to support local schools. Education reforms in 1995 allowed local districts more say in how their funds were spent. Texas provides public school for all children, regardless of their legal status. Some people feel that educating the children of illegal aliens is an unjustified tax burden. Many other Texans believe that if young illegal immigrants are barred from the public schools, they will never be able to rise above a life of poverty, that it is in the best interest of the state to educate all of the children living within its borders.

Providing a good education for its young people is one of the best ways for a state to cut down on the crime rate. In an effort to encourage more students to attend college, the state guarantees that students who graduate in the top 10 percent of their class will gain entrance to a state university or college. Some people complain that illegal aliens pay the same lower college tuition rates as legal residents. The legislature granted all Texas high school graduates the lower rate, but noncitizens have to be residents of the state for at least three years prior to graduation. They are also required to sign a statement that they will apply for permanent residency as soon as they are eligible.

Chapter Five
Making a Living

Texas's strong economy can be traced back to the first Spaniards who moved across the Rio Grande and established cattle ranches. More than one hundred years later, in the early 1800s, Anglo settlers arrived and filled the eastern part of the state with farms. Then, after the Civil War, people settled farther west and developed ranches in that part of the state. Texas remained an agricultural state until a single event changed everything.

RICHES OF THE EARTH

On January 10, 1901, an enormous explosion was heard as a column of oil belched from the ground under a drilling rig on Spindletop Hill near Beaumont. Until the monster well was capped nine days later, oil spewed out of the ground at a rate of one hundred thousand barrels per day. It was the biggest oil gusher the world had ever seen.

Hundreds of other wells were drilled in the area, and 17.5 million barrels of petroleum were pumped out of the hill in 1902. The United States became the world's largest producer of oil as a result of the Spindletop field. Dozens of future industry giants were formed during

The oil well—a classic symbol of West Texas.

the frenzy that followed, including Gulf Oil and Texaco (both now part of Chevron), and Humble and Mobil (both now part of Exxon). Later in the 1900s, other huge reservoirs of oil were discovered in East Texas, the Panhandle, and in the Permian Basin in West Texas.

New jobs came with the discovery of oil. Refineries were built to process massive quantities of petroleum, and thousands of people were hired to work. Almost overnight Texas went from an agricultural state to an industrial empire. By 1920 nearly one-third of the state's population lived in cities.

World War II brought a great demand for oil products to run machinery. For the next forty years, Texas's economy steadily grew. Then, the sudden drop in oil prices brought a recession in the mid-1980s. Many businesses went bankrupt. It took more than a decade for Houston, the center of Texas's oil and refining industry, to recover. Officials learned not to rely so heavily on a single source of state income. So leaders worked to create a more balanced economy. Oil and gas, once 25 percent of the state's revenue, accounted for only 6 percent in 2001.

GOODS AND SERVICES

Services—jobs people do at hotels, businesses, hospitals, schools, and the like—make up about one-quarter of Texas's gross state product. Wholesale and retail trade come next, followed by financial business such as banking, insurance, and real estate. Manufacture of products such as furniture, industrial machinery, electronic equipment, and food products make up a little less than one-fifth of the state's gross state product, while transportation and government jobs each amount to around 11 percent. Construction, mining, and agriculture are also important to the state, though they contribute lesser amounts.

Manufacturing is a key part of the state's economy.

TEXAS
BY
COUNTY

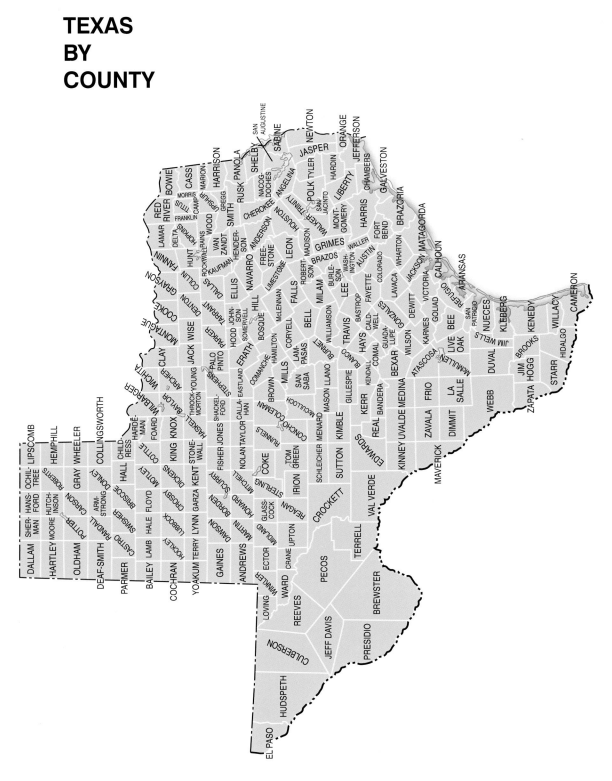

Manufactured items are sold not only within the state but to foreign countries as well. The Texas construction industry uses much of the concrete, gypsum, plaster, and lumber that the state produces. Foreign nations buy industrial machinery, computers, electronics, chemicals, and transportation equipment made in Texas.

Texas exports, the goods sold outside the state, amounted to $98.8 billion in 2003. The Port of Houston, which ships goods around the world, handles more foreign tonnage than any other port in the United States. To encourage trade, 129 countries maintain consulates in Texas, with 74 of them located in Houston.

Mexico is Texas's biggest trade partner. Texas produces 41 percent of all the goods that the United States sells to Mexico. Truck traffic has increased on Texas highways because of the North American Free Trade Agreement (NAFTA), established in 1994. The agreement allows goods to pass between countries in North America without fees being charged at the border. Approximately 4,700 plants in Mexico assemble American parts into products that are then shipped back to the United States.

Canada is the second-largest export destination for Texas goods, with Japan being third. Other Asian countries are top destinations as well.

AGRICULTURE

Even though most Texans don't work as farmers now, the state's size makes it the nation's leader in the number of farms and ranches and in the amount of land used for agriculture. In 2001 Texas ranked second in the nation in cash receipts from its farms and ranches. Two-thirds of that was from livestock—cattle, hogs, and sheep—and their related products. Texas has the largest number of cattle, sheep, and goats in the nation. It ranks first in wool and mohair (goat-hair) production. Some dairy products are produced as well.

Texas ranchers and farmers use modern communication systems to ensure their operations run smoothly.

Before the 1950s farms were small and generally family owned. Since then, they have become fewer, larger, more expensive to operate, and more productive. Irrigation allows production on land once too dry to support crops. Computers and other high-tech tools are used to manage farm operations. Texas A&M University System provides research and educational programs to help farmers take advantage of the mild climate, good soil, and excellent transportation systems in Texas. The result is that, in 2002, Texas agribusiness—everything related to the production, processing, and distribution of farm produce—amounted to about $28 billion.

Cotton is the major cash crop. For 120 years, Texas has led the nation in cotton production almost every year. Cottonseed, used as cattle feed, is a valuable by-product. Greenhouse and nursery plants have also grown in

2003 GROSS STATE PRODUCT: $813 BILLION

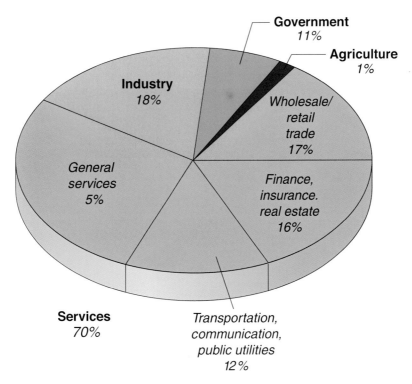

Government
11%

Agriculture
1%

Industry
18%

Wholesale/
retail
trade
17%

General
services
5%

Finance,
insurance.
real estate
16%

Services
70%

Transportation,
communication,
public utilities
12%

importance. Twenty percent of the roses grown in the United States are cultivated in Tyler.

Major Texas crops include corn, wheat, sorghum, hay, peanuts, and rice. Nuts such as pecans are raised commercially, with Texas sometimes surpassing Georgia as the top pecan producer. Vegetables grown in the state are not only sold as fresh produce, but some, such as tomatoes, bell peppers, and spinach, are canned or frozen.

UPS AND DOWNS

Texas's economy faced a bright future at the beginning of the new century. Then, in the fall of 2001, Enron, one of the world's largest energy traders, suddenly collapsed. Lawsuits were filed, but workers still lost paychecks and pension savings. The scandal brought hardship not only to businesses directly connected with Enron but to those with no direct link at all.

TEXAS WORKFORCE

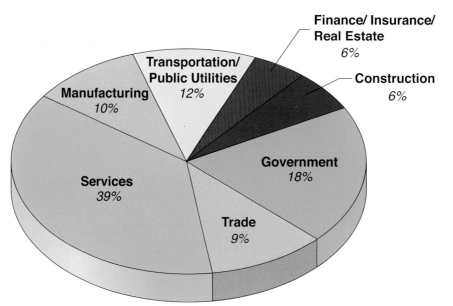

Finance/ Insurance/ Real Estate 6%

Construction 6%

Transportation/ Public Utilities 12%

Manufacturing 10%

Government 18%

Services 39%

Trade 9%

Longhorns, well-known symbols of Texas, adapted to life on the plains. They resisted disease and were able to thrive in the often harsh climate and terrain.

People had less money to spend. Businesses closed, causing the state to lose more jobs.

In spite of that, Texas has led all other states in the creation of jobs for more than ten years. People like to live in Texas because there is no state income tax. Even though the legislature faced a $9.9 million deficit in 2003, politicians did not consider an income tax because Texans have such strong feelings against it. To provide funds for state programs, residents pay a high rate of state sales taxes.

One controversial method of raising revenue for the state is the lottery. Its supporters point out the amount the state has received for education. Opponents object not only because they believe gambling is morally wrong but also because many of the tickets are bought by the poor, a group least able to afford to lose their money.

Tourism is also big business in Texas. Millions of tourists spend about $40 billion every year visiting the various sites spread across the second-largest state in the Union. Businesses are attracted to the state as well. Companies have moved their corporate headquarters to Texas, lured by the warm weather and the healthy business climate. In May 2003 *Forbes* magazine named Austin as the number one city in the nation to locate a business. The selection was based on factors such as the cost of doing business, the low crime rate, and the education level of the workforce. Dallas ranked number eight on the list.

Just like every other state, Texas has faced times when money is tight. But even in lean times, Texas's economy is impressive by its sheer size. If Texas were still an independent country, only about eight other nations would have an economy larger than the Lone Star State.

A farmers market stands in the shadow of Dallas skyscrapers. Tourism adds much wealth to the state economy each year.

Chapter Six

Travel through Texas

Some visitors to Texas enter the state in the northeastern corner near the place where the first U.S. settlers entered. Texarkana, as its name implies, is part in Texas and part in Arkansas.

DALLAS–FORT WORTH

About 150 miles west of Texarkana, sprawling suburbs surround the glass-and-steel buildings of downtown Dallas. Dallas started as just one log cabin in 1841, but today is a city of skyscrapers, museums, fine hotels, and big business. It is the home of the Neiman Marcus specialty store and the State Fair of Texas. A memorial honors President John F. Kennedy, who was assassinated there in 1963.

Next door in Irving is the stadium where the Dallas Cowboys football team plays. Nearby in Arlington the Texas Rangers baseball team attracts thousands of fans. Thirty miles west is Fort Worth, half the size of Dallas and very proud of its western heritage. The National Cowgirl Museum and Hall of Fame is there. In June, the Chisholm Trail

Hikers enjoy a front-row view of Casa Grande peak.

PLACES TO SEE

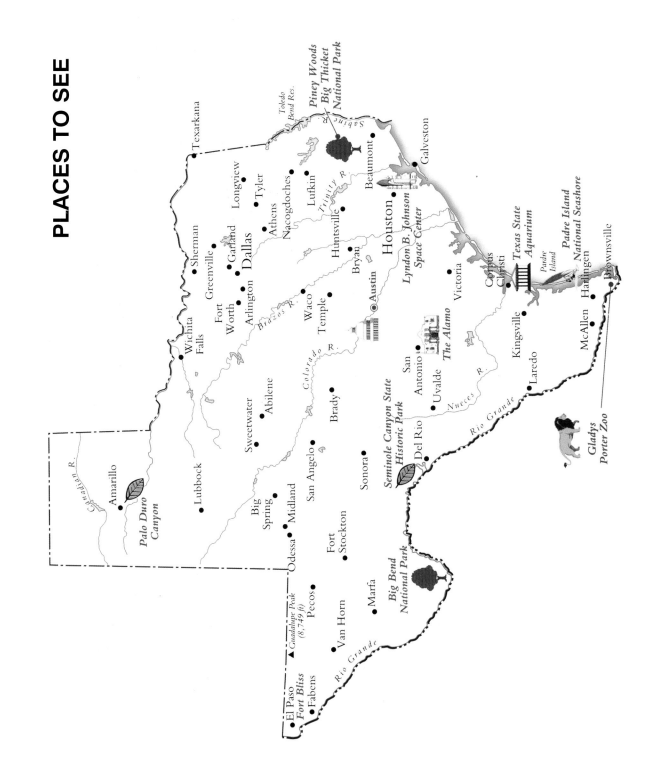

Toledo
Bend Res.

Piney Woods
Big Thicket
National Park

Texarkana

Sabine R.

Galveston

Longview

Tyler

Beaumont

Athens

Nacogdoches

Lufkin

Trinity R.

Houston

Sherman

Garland

Greenville

Dallas

Huntsville

Lyndon B. Johnson
Space Center

Texas State
Aquarium

Padre Island
National Seashore

Fort
Worth

Arlington

Bryan

Brazos R.

Austin

Victoria

Corpus
Christi

Padre
Island

Brownsville

Wichita
Falls

Waco

Temple

San
Antonio

The Alamo

Kingsville

Harlingen

McAllen

Colorado R.

Uvalde

Nueces R.

Laredo

Canadian R.

Amarillo

Palo Duro
Canyon

Lubbock

Sweetwater

Abilene

Brady

Rio Grande

Gladys
Porter Zoo

San Angelo

Sonora

Seminole Canyon State
Historic Park

Del Rio

Big
Spring

Midland

Fort
Stockton

Odessa

▲ *Guadalupe Peak*
(8,749 ft)

Pecos

Van Horn

Marfa

Big Bend
National Park

El Paso
Fort Bliss

Fabens

Rio Grande

Roundup is held in the Fort Worth Stockyards. The celebration begins with a trail drive and also features a chili cook-off, parade, and rodeo.

AUSTIN

Two hundred miles south of Dallas is the state capital. Named for Stephen F. Austin, the city is located on the banks of the Colorado River in a scenic, hilly part of Texas. Austin has been the capital of Texas since 1839. The state capitol building was completed in 1888. At the time of construction, a special railroad line was built to haul granite from a nearby quarry. By 1988 the one-hundred-year-old building was in need of major repair work. Also the state government had grown, and the legislators needed more office space. So a massive, $200-million project restored the fine old structure to its former beauty and added a huge underground extension.

Other Austin attractions include the University of Texas campus and the Congress Avenue Bridge. More than half a million Mexican free-tailed bats make their home under the bridge from March until November every year. In the evenings, people gather in the area to watch as clouds of bats fly into the night sky in search of insects. Austin has become a major music center as well, where musicians play country, rock, blues, and reggae each night.

SAN ANTONIO

One of Texas's most unique cities, San Antonio, is about 100 miles southwest of Austin. It began as the center of Spanish government of Texas. The Alamo, already in ruins when Texans were overrun by Mexican forces in 1836, draws visitors from around the world. A group of women, including Adina De Zavala and Clara Driscoll, saved the mission from being torn down. Their organization, Daughters of the Republic of Texas, owns and

The Alamo in San Antonio is a symbol of freedom that is known around the world.

cares for the Texas shrine. Visitors can walk through the chapel and long barracks, where Texans fought for their independence from Mexico.

A few blocks away, the meandering San Antonio River winds through the city. There are many restaurants and interesting shops along the River Walk. This promenade with its sight-seeing boats was built when a group of women convinced city fathers to develop the area rather than cover over the waterway with concrete. During the annual Fiesta, it is traditional for revelers to race up and down the Riverwalk, bashing each other with *cascarones,* which are eggshells filled with confetti.

THE PANHANDLE

Nearly 500 miles northwest of San Antonio, Amarillo sits on the flat High Plains. It is a city of modern buildings built on the profits of agriculture, oil, and cattle. The largest independent livestock auctions in the state, selling more than 300,000 head of cattle a year, are held in the Amarillo stockyards.

North of Amarillo, visitors sometimes tour the Alibates Flint Quarries National Monument on the Canadian River. Prehistoric inhabitants gathered the distinctive maroon-and-white flint for their arrowheads, spear points, and tools. Flint is an extremely hard rock. Park ranger Ed Day said, "The Indians could make almost any kind of tool or weapon with this rock. Flint is so hard that you can scratch your pocketknife with it."

In Canyon, 20 miles south of Amarillo, the Panhandle-Plains Historical Museum is the largest history museum in Texas. Nearby, visitors to Palo Duro Canyon can take a ride along the canyon bottom on the Sad Monkey Railroad or watch outdoor productions telling the story of the state.

Ancient arrowheads and other artifacts are valuable clues to a better understanding of Texas's native past. Wine-colored Alibates flint, quarried north of Amarillo, was prized for its color and traded far distances.

South of Amarillo, Midland and Odessa are Permian Basin oil towns that grew after 1923. Then in the 1940s, huge quantities of petroleum were discovered at a much greater depth. Midland is home to the Commemorative Air Force, an organization that restores and flies World War II aircraft. More than one hundred planes are on display in a museum that also features military uniforms and war memorabilia.

EL PASO AND THE RIO GRANDE

Sightseers travel west with little to greet them on the way to El Paso except scattered towns, big ranches, and a vast blue sky. This is the driest part of Texas. Nestled in a bowl of mountains, El Paso sits at the western tip of Texas, across the Rio Grande from its sister, Ciudad Juárez, Mexico. A park, Chamizal National Memorial, celebrates the peaceful end of a border dispute with Mexico. Also located in El Paso is Fort Bliss, which was established in 1848. There are several museums on the historic site that trace the history of the fort from frontier times. Today, twenty thousand American troops are stationed at Fort Bliss, the largest air-defense base in the United States.

The Rio Grande flows southeast from El Paso through desolate country, forming the boundary with Mexico. Residents cross back and forth across the border to work and shop. Both Spanish and English are spoken in the stores.

Many miles south of El Paso, from Presidio to Big Bend National Park, a winding road follows the river through picturesque scenery. Abandoned movie sets dot the area. Then the river slices through the mountain ranges of Big Bend National Park. More than one hundred years ago, an unidentified Mexican vaquero (cowboy) said that it was an area "where the rainbows wait for the rain, and the big river is kept in a stone box, and water runs uphill and mountains float in the air." The park has several hundred miles of trails for hiking or horseback riding. Rafters floating down the river emerge from the canyons of Big Bend and reach a stretch designated as the Rio Grande Wild and Scenic River.

As the Rio Grande continues on its southward path, it forms the Amistad Reservoir near Del Rio. This joint project of the United States and Mexico provides for water conservation and recreation. Nearby, Seminole Canyon State Park and Historic Site has rock shelters with ancient Native American paintings still visible on the stone walls. The many colorful pictographs, which are some of the oldest in the country, were painted more than four thousand years ago. The prehistoric artists made paint out of minerals that they had dug from the soil and then mixed with animal fat. Using their fingers, along with brushes made from plants, the early people painted animals, human figures, and weapons on the rocky surfaces under overhanging ledges.

The last stop on the path of the Rio Grande is Brownsville, located near the southern tip of the state. The river is almost dry at this point because so much water has been removed for irrigation. Palm trees and bougainvillea grow in the tropical air of the port city. In the Gladys Porter Zoo, which has been named one of the ten best zoos in the country, nearly two thousand birds, mammals, and reptiles are on display in natural settings that have no bars. Just across the border from Brownsville is the Mexican city of Matamoros. The two bridges that connect the cities are filled with tourists much of the time. Like other Mexican border towns, Matamoros lures shoppers with jewelry, pottery, wood carvings, and other objects.

The enormous King Ranch occupies several counties north of Brownsville. Farther up the seacoast, Corpus Christi is called "Sparkle City by the Sea." Tourists walk along the 2-mile seawall of Shoreline Drive,

Rafters in Santa Elena Canyon in Big Bend National Park.

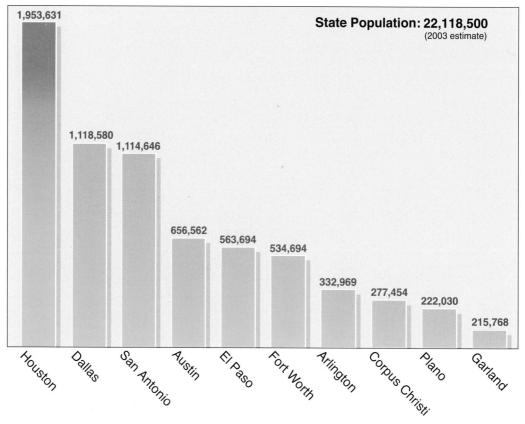

watching sailboats skim across the water of Corpus Christi Bay. Children throw bread crumbs to the clouds of hungry seagulls that squawk in the balmy air. Also facing the bay is the Texas State Aquarium, where visitors can watch sharks, rays, and tropical fish swim in huge saltwater tanks as they wind down "below the surface" of an offshore oil rig. The city has replicas of Columbus's three ships that sailed across the Atlantic to celebrate the five hundredth anniversary of the famous voyager's first trip to the New World. Docked nearby is the aircraft carrier *Lexington,* called the Blue Ghost because it was reported sunk so often during World War II.

The warm coastal waters and wide beaches of Texas's gulf coast attract visitors from all around.

Two hundred miles farther up the Texas coast is Galveston Island. The city of Galveston was once called the "Wall Street of the South" because of the commerce brought in by ships. Tourist come to swim, fish, and tour the old sailing ship *Elissa*, a remnant of Galveston's glory days. The city loves to celebrate and boasts one of the nation's biggest Mardi Gras celebrations.

About 50 miles north of Galveston is the sprawling city of Houston, the largest city in Texas. Houston was the first capital of Texas but was quickly replaced by Austin. After the devastating 1900 storm in Galveston, Buffalo Bayou was dredged to make Houston an inland port for oceangoing ships. Petrochemical plants light up the sky at night along the Houston Ship Channel. The city is also known for its ballet company and symphony, and its annual Houston Livestock Show and Rodeo is the largest in the world.

SAN JACINTO DAY

Every year the victory at San Jacinto is remembered with a living history celebration. One hundred fifty participants, dressed in leather britches and fringed boots, set up Texan and Mexican camps that reflect conditions in 1836. As the men sit around blazing fires, they polish nineteenth-century muskets, swords, and bayonets. At 4:30 in the afternoon, the Texans fire a cannon and advance on the Mexican camp to re-enact the eighteen-minute battle. To conclude the ceremonies, a tribute is read in English and Spanish, and a wreath is laid to honor all who died at the Battle of San Jacinto.

The sailing ship Elissa, *docked in Galveston, has been restored to its condition when it brought goods to the "Wall Street of the South" in the late 1800s.*

A young Alabama-Coushatta Indian displays the traditional garb of his people.

A few miles east of Houston, the tall San Jacinto Monument sits in a 1,000-acre historical park, marking the place where Texas and Mexican soldiers clashed on April 21, 1836. Central to the park is a 570-foot monument. Elevators inside the monument take visitors to the top for a look at the Houston ship channel and city skyline. The museum at the base features exhibits that trace Texas history from its earliest days to the present.

About 90 miles east of Houston, Beaumont, near the Louisiana border, is the site of the Spindletop oil gusher. North of there, the Alabama-Coushatta Indians make their home on a reservation near the Big Thicket. A drive through some of the four national forests brings

A lone canoeist paddles along Caddo Lake in Texas's Piney Woods.

the traveler to Nacogdoches, one of the oldest towns in the state. Continuing north, visitors pass through more of the Piney Woods to return to the place where the tour started.

Most Texans live in big cities and their suburbs, but many others live in small towns. Some towns, such as Mentone with its population of seventeen, are very tiny. Mentone is the county seat of Loving County, whose eighty-seven residents make it the least populated county in the nation. In central Texas, President George W. Bush chose a ranch outside of Crawford, population 705, to be his home. City dwellers, farmers, ranchers, and small-town residents—they are all proud of their state and proud to be called Texans.

The sheer 1,500-foot-high walls of Santa Elena Canyon flank the Rio Grande as it marks the boundary between Texas and Mexico.

THE FLAG: Called the Lone Star Flag, it has three parts: a white horizontal stripe, a red horizontal stripe, and a blue vertical stripe with a white five-pointed star in its center. The red stands for bravery, the white for purity, and the blue for loyalty. Between 1836 and 1845, Texas was a separate country called the Republic of Texas, and this was its official flag. It was adopted by the Third Congress of the Republic on January 25, 1839. When Texas joined the United States in 1845, the Lone Star Flag became the state flag. It is from this flag that Texas got its nickname.

THE SEAL: The seal was first adopted on December 10, 1836, as the Great Seal of the Republic of Texas. When Texas became a state, it was changed slightly and adopted as the official state seal, which is still in use today.

State Survey

Statehood: December 29, 1845

Origin of Name: The word *Texas*, or *Tejas* in Spanish, comes from a Caddo word meaning "friends" or "allies."

Nickname: The Lone Star State

Capital: Austin

Motto: Friendship

Bird: Mockingbird

Large animal: Texas longhorn

Small animal: Armadillo

Fish: Guadalupe bass

Flower: Bluebonnet

Tree: Pecan

Gem: Texas blue topaz

Folk Dance: Square dance

Fruit: Texas red grapefruit

Dish: Chili

Armadillo

Cow in a field of bluebonnets

TEXAS, OUR TEXAS

"Texas, Our Texas" was adopted by the Texas legislature as the official state song in May 1929.

Words by Gladys Y. Marsh and William J. Marsh
Music by William Marsh

Tex - as, our Tex - as! all hail the might - y State!

Tex - as, our Tex - as! So won - der - ful and great!

Bold - est and grand - est, with - stand - ing ev - 'ry test; O,

Em - pire wide and glo - rious, You stand su - preme - ly blest.

God bless you, Tex - as! And keep you brave and strong, That

you may grow in power and worth, Thro' - out the a - ges long.

Highest Point: Guadalupe Peak in far West Texas at 8,749 feet

Lowest Point: The Gulf of Mexico, at sea level

Area: 261,914 square miles, 7 percent of the area of the United States

Greatest Distance North to South: 801 miles

Greatest Distance East to West: 773 miles

Borders: Oklahoma to the north; Arkansas and Louisiana to the east; the Gulf of Mexico to the southeast; New Mexico to the west; Mexico to the southwest

Hottest Recorded Temperature: 120°F at Seymour on August 12, 1936, and at Monahans on June 28, 1994

Coldest Recorded Temperature: -23°F at Tulia on February 12, 1899, and at Seminole on February 8, 1933

Average Annual Precipitation: 27.21 inches

Major Rivers: Rio Grande, Red, Sabine, Colorado, Brazos, Trinity, Canadian, Pecos, San Antonio, Guadalupe, Neches, Nueces

Major Lakes: Caddo Lake in northeastern Texas is the only major natural lake. Impounded rivers form Amistad, Falcon, Richland-Chambers, Sam Rayburn, and Toledo Bend reservoirs as well as lakes named Livingston, Texoma, and Travis.

Trees: black gum, cottonwood, cypress, elm, hickory, horseapple, huisache, juniper, live oak, magnolia, mesquite, oak, palm, pecan, pine, piñon pine, ponderosa pine, post oak, sweet gum, Texas mountain laurel, tupelo, walnut

Wild Plants: bluebonnet, bluestem, buffalo grass, Indiangrass, Indian paintbrush, Mexican hat, ocotillo, prickly pear, ragweed, saltgrass, sideoats grama, tumblegrass, yucca

Animals: alligator, nine-banded armadillo, badger, bat, beaver, bighorn sheep, black bear, black-tailed jackrabbit, bobcat, cougar (mountain lion), coyote, gopher, gray fox, horned lizard, javelina, kit fox, mink, mole, mule deer, muskrat, opossum, prairie dog, raccoon, skunk, snake, squirrel, white-tailed deer, yellow-haired porcupine

Birds: great horned owl, hawk, mottled duck, quail, roseate spoonbill, sandhill crane, sparrow, wild turkey, wood stork

Fish: catfish, largemouth bass, sunfish

Endangered Plants: black lace cactus, Texas wild-rice, Navasota ladies'-tresses, Texas snowbells, Texas trailing phlox, Texas poppy-mallow, large-fruited sand verbena

Endangered Animals:

greater long-nosed bat, black-footed ferret, jaguar, jaguarundi, West Indian manatee, ocelot, finback whale, gray wolf, red wolf, whooping crane, Eskimo curlew, peregrine falcon, south-western willow flycatcher, eastern brown pelican, Attwater's greater prairie chicken, interior least tern, black-capped vireo,

Ocelot

ivory-billed woodpecker, red-cockaded woodpecker, Bachman's warbler, golden-cheeked warbler, Atlantic hawksbill sea turtle, leatherback sea turtle, Kemp's ridley sea turtle, Barton Springs salamander, Texas blind salamander, fountain darter, Big Bend gambusia, San Marcos gambusia, Rio Grande silvery minnow, Comanche Springs pupfish, Leon Springs pupfish

TIMELINE

Texas History

1528 Spanish explorer Álvar Núñez Cabeza de Vaca and Moroccan slave Estevanico are shipwrecked on the Gulf Coast

1541 Francisco Vásquez de Coronado discovers Palo Duro Canyon

1681 Spanish Franciscan missionaries establish Ysleta, oldest European settlement in Texas

1685 René-Robert Cavelier, Sieur de la Salle, builds Fort Saint Louis

1700s Comanches move into Texas

1718 Spanish Franciscan missionaries establish the Alamo

1758 Comanches destroy San Sabá Mission

1821 Texas becomes part of Mexico; first settlers arrive at Stephen F. Austin's land grant

1835 Texans challenge Mexicans at Gonzales

1836 Texans declare independence from Mexico; Mexicans defeat Texans at the Alamo; Texans win victory at San Jacinto; the Republic of Texas is declared

1839 All Native Americans, except for the Alabama-Coushatta, are ordered to leave the Republic of Texas

1845 Texas joins the United States

1846 Mexican War begins in Texas

1848 Treaty of Guadalupe Hidalgo

1850 Compromise of 1850 creates present-day Texas boundaries

1853 The first Texas railroad begins operation

1861 Texas joins the Confederacy in the Civil War

1865 Slaves in Texas are emancipated

1875 Comanches led by Quanah Parker are defeated by U.S. Cavalry troops

1900 Galveston hurricane kills six thousand people

1901 Anthony Lucas discovers oil at Spindletop

1919 Texas approves women's right to vote

1925 Miriam "Ma" Ferguson becomes the first woman elected governor of Texas

1932 Texan "Babe" Didrikson wins two gold medals and one silver medal at the Olympics

1941–1945 During World War II, 750,000 Texans serve in the military

1950 Herman Marion Sweatt becomes the first African American admitted to the University of Texas Law School

1958 Jack Kilby invents the integrated circuit at Texas Instruments

1961 The National Aeronautics and Space Administration (NASA) opens the Manned Spacecraft Center in Houston

1963 President John F. Kennedy is assassinated in Dallas

1965 The Astrodome, the world's first air-conditioned football and baseball stadium, opens in Houston. It is replaced in 2002 by Reliant Stadium.

1986 Texas celebrates its sesquicentennial (150 years) of independence

1990 Ann Richards is the second woman to be elected governor

1993 A fifty-one-day standoff between federal law-enforcement officers and Branch Davidians ends in fiery disaster at the cult's compound in Waco

1994 George W. Bush is elected governor

2000 George W. Bush resigns as governor to assume the presidency

2001 Tropical storm Allison causes $5.2 billion in damage in southeastern Texas

2003 The space shuttle *Columbia* breaks up over Texas just before a landing attempt

2004 George W. Bush is elected to a second term as president of the United States

Manufactured Products: petroleum products, aeronautical equipment, electronics, computers, paper, furniture, glass, rubber, lumber, plywood, metal products, industrial machinery, concrete, bricks, textiles, food and dairy products

Agricultural Products: cotton and cottonseed, grain sorghum, rice, wheat, corn, rye, oats, barley, sugarcane, hay, peanuts, soybeans, sunflowers, flaxseed, vegetables, pecans, citrus fruit, peaches, beef and beef products, poultry and eggs, hogs, sheep and wool, goats and mohair, horses and mules

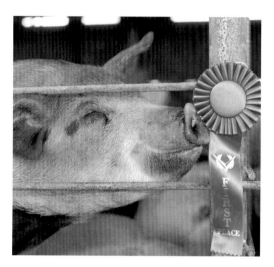

Hogs

Natural Resources: lumber, oil, natural gas, limestone, sandstone, sand and gravel, cement materials, coal, clay, sulfur, gypsum, salt, granite, marble

Business and Trade: oil and gas production and refining, construction, transportation, wholesale and retail trade, tourism, banking, insurance, communications, health care and health research, computer industry, state government, aerospace, business services, hotel industry, farming, ranching

Martin Luther King, Jr.'s birthday, observed on the third Monday in January, honors the African-American minister, nonviolent civil rights leader, and Nobel Peace Prize winner. State employees, federal employees, and students enjoy a holiday from work and school.

Texas Independence Day, March 2, is a state holiday celebrated throughout Texas with picnics, barbecues, parades, and fireworks after sundown.

San Jacinto Day, April 21, is a state holiday celebrating the Texas army's victory at the Battle of San Jacinto, led by General Sam Houston. This battle established Texas's independence from Mexico. Many Texans visit the San Jacinto Battleground and San Jacinto Monument near Houston on this holiday.

Cinco de Mayo, May 5, is celebrated throughout Texas and Mexico. It marks Mexico's final rejection of European rule in 1862. Parades are held in many cities in Texas including San Antonio, Corpus Christi, Dallas, and Houston.

Juneteenth or Emancipation Day, a state holiday commemorating the freeing of slaves, is celebrated on June 19. Texans of African descent traditionally take a holiday from work to celebrate this day with family reunions and picnic feasts. It was not a legal holiday, however, until 1980.

Lyndon B. Johnson's birthday, August 27, is a state holiday honoring this native Texan, the thirty-sixth president of the United States. Texans can make the scenic drive to Johnson City in central Texas and visit Johnson's boyhood home, then picnic in a nearby state park.

Cinco De Mayo celebration

Fiestas Patrias, September 16, is Mexican Independence Day, celebrating the anniversary of the first move to end European dominance in Mexico. The celebration begins on September 15 each year, when Mexican Texans have large parties, dress in traditional clothing, eat special foods, and dance and sing to Mexican music.

The State Fair of Texas is held every year during September and October in Dallas at the huge Fair Park fairgrounds, whose stadium is also the site of the annual Cotton Bowl. Thousands of Texans and visitors attend the festivities and take part in the amusements and enjoy foods such as hot buttered corn on the cob.

Oktoberfest is celebrated in early October, especially in the central Texas German communities of New Braunfels and Fredericksburg. Oktoberfests began in the mid-1800s with large gatherings of German-American singing societies called *Saengerfests* and *Volkfests.* Today, Texans of all backgrounds gather for several days to celebrate German culture, especially German music, dancing, and food.

El Día de los Muertos (Day of the Dead), November 1 and 2, is the Mexican version of the Roman Catholic All Saints Day or All Souls Day. It is a special Mexican mix of pre-Columbian homage to ancestors and Catholic ritual. In Austin, the holiday is marked with a special parade down Congress Avenue. It includes skeleton-decorated floats, ceremonial altars, and "low-rider" vehicles.

The State Fair of Texas

Alvin Ailey (1931–1989), African-American dancer and choreographer, was born in Rogers but moved to Los Angeles at age twelve. He began formal dance training in high school and after college founded the Alvin Ailey American Dance Theatre in New York. In 1965 his company made a successful tour of Europe, receiving an amazing sixty-one curtain calls in Hamburg, Germany.

Stephen F. Austin (1793–1836) obtained a land grant from Mexico in 1821 and founded a colony in Texas of three hundred Anglo Americans. As settlements grew, he tried to keep peace between the Mexican government and the Anglo settlers. But after he was wrongly imprisoned in Mexico, he helped the Texas Revolution and was elected the first secretary of state of the new Texas Republic. The city of Austin was named in his honor.

Stephen F. Austin

Gail Borden (1801–1874), a New Yorker, settled in Texas in 1829. He worked on several unsuccessful inventions but went bankrupt and returned to the Northeast. In 1856 he received a patent for condensing milk in a vacuum and opened a plant. When the Civil War broke out, Borden's canned milk, which wouldn't spoil, was in demand by the Union army. Later the general public also began buying it, and Borden returned to Texas. A town and a county there are named for him.

Carol Burnett (1933–   ), television comedian and film actor, was born in San Antonio. She first gained national attention on TV's *Garry Moore Show* in 1956. For eleven years (1967–1978), she hosted her own comedy-based television program, *The Carol Burnett Show,* and became a household name. Her film credits include *A Wedding, The Four Seasons, Annie,* and the Emmy Award–winning *Friendly Fire.*

George H. W. Bush (1924–   ) was one of the navy's youngest pilots in World War II, in which he received the Distinguished Flying Cross for bravery in action. Known for his desire to mold the United States into "a kinder and gentler nation," he served two terms as a U.S. representative from Texas. He later was appointed to several key government positions, including ambassador to the United Nations and director of the Central Intelligence Agency. Serving as Ronald Reagan's vice president from 1981 to 1988, he was elected president in 1988 and served for one term.

George W. Bush (1946–   ) is a graduate of Yale and Harvard universities. After finishing his schooling, Bush began a career in the energy industry, worked on his father's 1988 presidential campaign, and was one of a group of investors that purchased the baseball franchise the Texas Rangers in 1989. Elected governor of Texas twice in 1994 and 1998, he resigned during his second term after a successful bid for the presidency in 2000. Bush was then re-elected to a second term in 2004.

Earl Campbell (1955–   ), born in Tyler, gained fame as a running back with the University of Texas Longhorns. In his four years at UT he rushed for 4,444 yards and was named to the all-conference team four times. The Texas legislature officially designated him a "state legend," and he won the Heisman Memorial Trophy in 1977. He was elected to the Pro Football Hall of Fame in 1991.

Henry G. Cisneros (1947–   ), statesman born in San Antonio, gained prominence as the first Hispanic mayor of a major U.S. city when he was elected in San Antonio in 1981. In 1993 he was appointed Secretary of Housing and Urban Development (HUD) by President Bill Clinton.

Van Cliburn (1934–   ), pianist from Kilgore, won a statewide piano competition at age twelve. At thirteen, he made his debut with the Houston Symphony, and the next year he played at Carnegie Hall in New York. In 1958 he became the first American to win the gold medal at the International Tchaikovsky Competition in Russia. He returned to a ticker-tape parade in New York and a reception at the White House from President Dwight Eisenhower.

Horton Foote (1916–   ), playwright and screenwriter, was born in Wharton. He received his first Academy Award in 1962 for writing the screenplay of *To Kill a Mockingbird*. He won his second Oscar in 1983 for his screenplay *Tender Mercies*. He also wrote screenplays for *The Trip to Bountiful, 1918,* and *On Valentine's Day,* all set in Texas. In 1995 he won the Pulitzer Prize for his play *The Young Man from Atlanta.*

John Nance Garner (1868–1967) of Uvalde was elected to the U.S. House of Representatives in 1902. He served there for thirty years. Known as "Cactus Jack," he became speaker of the House in 1931 and U.S. vice president in 1932, when Franklin D. Roosevelt became president. During his two terms as vice president, Garner pushed New Deal legislation through Congress.

Henry B. Gonzalez (1916–2000) was born in San Antonio. In 1956 he became the first Mexican American elected to the state senate since 1846. In 1961 he became the first Mexican American elected from Texas to the U.S. House of Representatives. At age seventy-eight in 1994, while serving his thirty-third year in Congress, Gonzalez accepted the Profile of Courage award, the only Texan ever to win it.

Henry B. Gonzalez

Oveta Culp Hobby (1905–1995) of Houston became the first director of the Women's Army Corps (WACs) in 1942. She was the first woman to attain the rank of colonel and to receive the army's Distinguished Service Medal. In the 1950s she was the first secretary of the Department of Health, Education, and Welfare. In 1964, after the death of her husband, she took his job as publisher of *The Houston Post*. She was the first woman elected director of the American Society of Newspaper Editors.

Ben Hogan (1912–1997) of Fort Worth started his golfing career as a caddie at age eleven. He electrified the golf world in 1946 when he won several major tournaments and took first place among money winners. He remained on top for ten years, winning the U.S. Open four times, even after an auto accident almost killed him in 1949. In 1950 a commission of sports writers named him one of the greatest golfers of the twentieth century.

Buddy Holly (1936–1959), born in Lubbock, was a songwriter and pioneer of rock and roll music. He had a strong and widespread influence on musicians such as the Beatles and Eric Clapton. Holly and his band, the Crickets, were among the first white rock bands to play their own songs. Holly wrote most of their hits, including "That'll Be the Day," "Peggy Sue," "Rave On," and "Maybe Baby." He died in a plane crash at age twenty-three.

Sam Houston (1793-1863) first came to Texas in 1832. He was soon caught up in the fight for Texas independence. As the commander of the small outnumbered Texas army, he won the Battle of San Jacinto. He was the Texas Republic's first president and, after Texas joined the Union, he served as a U.S. senator. Elected governor in 1859, he opposed Texas secession from the Union. When the Civil War broke out, he retired to Huntsville, where his home is now preserved as a museum.

John Arthur "Jack" Johnson (1878–1946) was a prizefighter born in Galveston. He was boxing's first African-American heavyweight champion of the world. He won the title in 1908 in Sydney, Australia, and

John Arthur "Jack" Johnson

remained world champion for seven years. His career included eighty wins, seven losses, and fourteen draws. He died following an automobile accident in North Carolina.

Lady Bird Johnson (1912–   ), born in Karnack, was First Lady to President Lyndon B. Johnson and the force behind the Highway Beautification Act passed by Congress in 1965. She founded the National Wildflower Research Center near Austin in 1982. In 1993 she presided over the ground-breaking ceremony for the center's new 42-acre site. It is the only nonprofit environmental organization dedicated to the study, preservation, and replanting of native plants.

Lyndon Baines Johnson (1908–1973), born near Stonewall, became an influential member of the U.S. House of Representatives and the Senate. As vice president, he became president after the assassination of President John F. Kennedy in 1963. During his presidency, LBJ used his power gained from years in Congress to pass many civil rights programs. They include the Civil Rights Act of 1964 and the Voting Rights Act of 1965. After losing popularity because of the Vietnam War, he did not seek a second term and retired to his Texas ranch.

Tommy Lee Jones (1946–   ), an actor born in San Saba, attended Harvard University on scholarship. He got his start acting in the early 1970s in *One Life to Live*, a television soap opera. In 1976 film work took him to Hollywood, where he earned enough to buy a ranch in Texas. He won an Emmy Award for *The Executioner's Song* and an Oscar for *The Fugitive*. Other film credits include *JFK, The Client, Blue Sky,* and *Blown Away.*

Scott Joplin (1868–1917), born in Cave Springs near Texarkana, was the son of a freed slave. He is credited with inventing ragtime music. He composed more than five hundred pieces of music, including a ballet and two operas. But his best-known tunes are "rags," or ragtime songs. His composition "The Entertainer" revived ragtime in 1973, when it was the theme of the Oscar-winning film *The Sting*. Although Joplin died in poverty, never to know fame during his lifetime, he was awarded a Pulitzer Prize in 1976 for his contributions to American music.

Barbara Jordan (1936–1996), born in Houston, was awarded the Medal of Freedom, the nation's highest civilian honor, in 1994. She began her political career in 1966, when she became the first black woman elected to the Texas senate. In 1972 she was elected as a U.S. representative, and she won national recognition serving on the Judiciary Committee during the investigation of the Watergate scandal. In her final years, she was a professor at the Lyndon B. Johnson School of Public Affairs at the University of Texas, Austin.

Barbara Jordan

Larry McMurtry (1936–   ), born in Wichita Falls, has written many best-selling novels. Among them are *Horseman Pass By, The Last Picture Show, Terms of Endearment,* and *Texasville*—all of which have been made into films. His Western novel *Lonesome Dove* won the 1986 Pulitzer Prize for fiction and was also made into a television film.

Audie Murphy (1924–1971), born in Farmersville, was the most decorated soldier in World War II. He won the Medal of Honor, the Distinguished Service Cross, and the Purple Heart. When he returned from the war in 1945, not yet twenty-one years old, he was greeted by parades all over Texas. Murphy wrote a best-selling book about his war experiences titled *To Hell and Back* and starred in several Hollywood films in the 1940s and 1950s. He died in an airplane crash.

Willie Nelson (1933–   ), born in Abbott, began his songwriting career in Nashville. His hit songs earned him a spot in the Nashville Songwriters Hall of Fame. Since returning to Texas in 1972, he has contributed to the growth and popularity of Texas music through his personal appearances, hit albums, and gold records such as "Blue Eyes Crying in the Rain." Nelson has sponsored music festivals to benefit farmers, hosted many famous Fourth of July picnics, and starred in films.

Willie Nelson

Quanah Parker (1847–1911), Comanche chief, was the son of Chief Peta Nocona and captive white woman Cynthia Ann Parker, who lived with the Comanches for twenty-four years. Quanah became the last great Comanche war chief at age nineteen, leading his people first in a war against the settlers, then during peacetime after surrendering in 1875. He went to Washington, D.C., for the inauguration of President Theodore Roosevelt and negotiated with the U.S. government on behalf of Indians.

H. Ross Perot (1930–   ), born in Texarkana, was named the richest person in Texas in 1993. His net worth then was estimated at $3.5 billion. He amassed his fortune in the computer industry, founding Electronic Data Systems (EDS) in 1962, which he later sold. In 1988 he founded Perot Systems, which now competes with EDS. Perot gained national attention during his unsuccessful $60-million campaign for president in 1992.

Katherine Anne Porter (1890–1980), short story writer and novelist, was born in Indian Creek. She was best known for her brilliant short stories until 1962, when her novel *Ship of Fools* appeared. It was made into a feature film with an all-star cast. She won the Pulitzer Prize in 1966 for *The Collected Stories*. She also wrote *Flowering Judas; Pale Horse, Pale Rider;* and *The Leaning Tower.*

Robert Rauschenberg (1925–   ), an artist born in Port Arthur, became a painter after serving in the navy during World War II. He studied art at the Art Students League in New York City and had his first one-man show there in 1951. Before age thirty he shocked the art world with his "combines," sculptural works made from found objects and paint. (One was a stuffed goat with a rubber tire around its middle.) From 1960 on he made mainly paintings and collages, becoming a world-renowned force in modern art.

Sam Rayburn (1882–1961), known as "Mr. Sam," grew up on a farm and practiced law in Bonham. In 1912 he was elected to the U.S. House of Representatives. He was re-elected twenty-four times and served for almost forty-nine years. In the 1930s he helped create New Deal legislation. He became speaker of the house in 1940 and held the post for seventeen years, also a record. A staunch Democrat, Rayburn won support for his policies from members of both parties, and he was one of the most powerful speakers in U.S. history.

Ann Richards (1933–   ), born in Lakeview, became in 1982 the first woman to be elected state treasurer. In 1988 she captured the public eye by delivering the keynote address at the Democratic convention. Elected governor of Texas in 1990, the second woman to hold that office, she appointed many Hispanics, blacks, and women to state offices. She lost her 1994 bid for re-election to George W. Bush, son of the former president.

Ann Richards

Nolan Ryan (1947–   ), baseball pitcher, was born in Refugio. On May 1, 1991, he pitched his seventh career no-hitter—setting a record in baseball history—while playing for the Texas Rangers against the Toronto Blue Jays. The native Texan also holds the world's record for the most strikeouts (5,714) and the most walks: 2,795 between 1968 and 1993. He was inducted into the Baseball Hall of Fame in 1999.

Lee Trevino (1939–), born in Dallas, was an accomplished golfer by age seventeen. After service in the marines, he played in his first Professional Golfers' Association (PGA) meet in 1966. In 1967 he was named Rookie of the Year. In 1968 he won the U.S. Open championship, setting a record as the first player to win with four below-par rounds. After a slump early in 1971, he came back later that year to be the first player ever to win the U.S., Canadian, and British opens in one year.

Tommy Tune (1939–), choreographer and director, was born in Houston. Unusually tall for a dancer, he was a standout in Broadway musicals such as *Bye Bye Birdie* and *My One and Only.* He soon went from dancing to choreography and directed *Nine, Grand Hotel,* and *The Will Rogers Follies,* all major hits. By 1994, when he had won a total of nine Tony Awards, Tune had established himself as one of America's most successful choreographers and musical directors

Victorio (1825–1880), Mimbreno Apache chief, was the last Native American leader in the nineteenth century to wage war against Texas. In 1878 a special regiment of the U.S. Cavalry was sent to the Trans Pecos region of West Texas to stop Victorio's raids on white settlements, both there and in Mexico. He escaped capture for two years, but in 1880 the Mexican Army, which had joined the chase, found and killed him.

Mildred "Babe" Didrikson Zaharias (1911–1956), an athlete, grew up in Beaumont. She got the nickname "Babe" (after Babe Ruth) while hitting home runs in sandlot baseball, and she also played basketball. In a national track meet in 1932, she won the team championship—all by herself. At the Olympic Games in Los Angeles that year, she won three medals and set two world records. As a professional golfer she won every major golf title between 1940 and 1950. Before dying from cancer, Babe played benefits for cancer research.

TOUR THE STATE

Amon Carter Museum of Western Art, Fort Worth, displays one of the nation's best collections of western art and photography. Nearby is the Kimball Art Museum, which shows modern American and European art in an unusual and award-winning building.

Sundance Square, Fort Worth, boasts a luxury hotel, restaurants, and shops in restored old buildings downtown. The site is named for the Sundance Kid, who in 1898 lived in this neighborhood with his side-kick Butch Cassidy and their Hole in the Wall Gang. In those days, the area's streets were dotted with saloons and dance halls, which entertained the famous gunslingers.

Caddoan Mounds State Historical Park, near Alto, is a village site of the Caddo tribe, which inhabited East Texas beginning about 800 C.E.. It is thought that the Caddos became extinct because of diseases brought by Europeans. The park covers almost 94 acres and includes two temple mounds, a burial mound, rebuilt dwellings, an information center, and educational hiking trails.

Big Thicket National Preserve, East Texas, called the "biological crossroads of North America," includes 97,000 acres that are home to many different plants and animals. It was made an International Biosphere

Reserve by the United Nations (UNESCO). There are eight hiking trails, ranging in length from a half mile to 18 miles, winding through a variety of forest communities that show the Big Thicket's diversity.

Alabama-Coushatta Reservation, Livingston, has been maintained since 1854, when Sam Houston requested that the land be set aside for these two Indian groups. A museum displays their culture and history, and summer visitors can also see live performances of dances in traditional costume and an official powwow ceremony.

Lyndon B. Johnson Space Center, Houston, is the mission control center from which U.S. space flights are directed. At the visitor center, a $70 million entertainment and education complex, tourists see displays of spacecraft, historic space equipment, and rocks taken from the moon, as well as videos and interactive multimedia about NASA.

Padre Island National Seashore, the Gulf Coast, is an 80-mile stretch of barrier island noted for sandy beaches, excellent fishing, and its many birds and sea animals. Five miles of the beach are open to camping, and there is an annual festival in mid-November for bird-watchers.

The Texas Ranger Hall of Fame and Museum, Waco, presents 150 years of history about the legendary Texas Rangers. On display are old guns and other objects used by the famous law enforcers.

The State Capitol, Austin, is modeled after the United States Capitol in Washington, D.C., but it is the tallest capitol in the United States.

The stately building is made of native pink granite and is surrounded by a tree-studded lawn. There are regular guided tours of the recently restored building and its historic treasures. The governor's mansion is across the street.

Elisabet Ney Museum, Austin, is a National Historic Site. In the 1800s it was the home and sculpture studio of one of the state's best-known artists, Elisabet Ney, a native of Germany. Her statues grace the capitol of Texas and the U.S. capitol in Washington, D.C. Many of her sculptures are also on view in the museum.

The Alamo, San Antonio, probably the best-known building in the state, has become a symbol of Texas. During the Texas Revolution, the Mexican Army defeated a small group of Texans defending this small fort. It was originally a Spanish mission. Today the Alamo is a museum and shrine in the care of the Daughters of the Republic of Texas. On guided tours, visitors can see actual belongings of the rebels who died there, including the famous knife of James Bowie.

Big Bend National Park, West Texas, was established in 1944. It is located in the great bend of the Rio Grande, the international boundary between the United States and Mexico. The park contains 801,163 acres of spectacular mountain and desert scenery, including unusual geological structures and the Chisos Mountains. Campsites are open year-round.

Ysleta Mission, El Paso, is Texas's oldest mission, built in 1681–1682 by Tiguas who had been converted to Christianity by Spanish missionaries.

It is part of the Tigua Reservation. Visitors today can see the sparkling rebuilt mission with its silver dome, as well as some of the remaining adobe walls of the original building.

Ysleta Mission

Find Out More

If you want to learn more about Texas, look for the following in your library or video store:

BOOKS

Adams, Simon, and David Murdoch. *Texas.* New York: DK Publishing, 2003.

Alter, Judy. *Texas.* Berkeley Heights, NJ: Enslow, 2002.

Bredeson, Carmen. *The Spindletop Gusher.* Brookfield, CT: Millbrook, 1996.

Garland, Sherry. *Voices of the Alamo.* Gretna, LA: Pelican Press, 2004.

Heinrichs, Ann. *Texas.* New York: Children's Press, 1999.

Sievert, Teri. *Texas.* Mankato, MN: Capstone, 2003.

Wade, Mary Dodson. *Texas.* 6 vols. Chicago: Heinemann, 2004.

VIDEOS

James Michener's Texas. Republic Studios, 1992. DVD, 2002.

Lonesome Dove. Cabin Fever Entertainment, 1992.

Texas Rangers: Manhunters of the Old West. A&E Home Video, 1994.

WEB SITES

On the Internet, go to the State of Texas home page at http://www.state.tx.us on the World Wide Web. You will find pictures, information, and suggestions for further research about the state.

The site of the Texas Almanac can be reached at http://www.texas almanac.com

The official site for Texas tourism is http://www.traveltex.com

The home page of the Texas Parks and Wildlife Department can be reached at http://www.tpwd.state.tx.us—click on the link, "Remember Texas brochure" for additional information.

The links "About Texas" and "Travel and Recreation" truly put, as this site claims, Texas at Your Fingertips. Go to http://www.state.tx.us

ABOUT THE AUTHORS

Carmen Bredeson worked as a librarian before turning to writing. To research this book, she and her husband, Larry, traveled from their home in Katy, Texas, to parts of the state they had never seen. She has also written histories of the Spindletop gusher and the siege of the Alamo as well as biographies of Henry Cisneros, George W. Bush, Laura Bush, and Ruth Bader Ginsburg.

Mary Dodson Wade spent twenty-five years as an elementary school librarian. Now writing full-time, she has produced more than forty books for young readers. Many of them are about Texas. She lives in Houston with her husband, and they both love to travel—across Texas and around the world.

Index

Page numbers in **boldface** are illustrations and charts.